Bolton Wanderers, An A–Z

by Dean Hayes

Palatine Books, 1994

Bolton Wanderers, An A–Z

by Dean Hayes

Palatine Books, 1994

Bolton Wanderers, An A–Z
by Dean Hayes

Published by Palatine Books,
an imprint of Carnegie Publishing Ltd,
18 Maynard Street, Preston

Text copyright © Dean Hayes, 1994
Illustrations copyright © see List of Illustrations

Typeset in Monotype Ehrhardt by Carnegie Publishing, Preston
Printed in the UK by T. Snape & Co., Preston

British Library Cataloguing-in-Publication Data
A CIP catalogue record for this book is available from the British Library

ISBN 1-874181-13-6

Contents

Abandoned Matches

An abandoned match may be defined as one which is called off by the referee, *while it is in progress*, because conditions do not permit it to be completed.

Generally speaking, far fewer matches are abandoned in modern times because if there is some doubt about the ability to play the full game, the match is more likely to be postponed.

On Boxing Day 1882 with Nottingham Forest leading the Wanderers 3–1, the referee gave some indifferent decisions which resulted in the Forest players leaving the field and refusing to return! On Christmas Day 1885, Bolton were leading Great Lever 2–1 at Woodside. The crowd began fighting and this spread to the players, leaving the officials no option but to abandon the game.

James Turner was the centre of a furore which saw the abandonment of a Lancashire Cup tie at Bury in March 1893, when the crowd rushed on to attack him after he was involved in a fracas with an opponent.

On New Year's Day 1979, Peter Reid broke his leg in a collision with Everton goalkeeper George Wood on a snowbound Burnden Park pitch, the game later being abandoned.

The last game at Burnden Park to be abandoned was in 1989 when a waterlogged pitch saw off the game with Wigan Athletic.

Accrington

A different club from the Accrington Stanley team which joined the League in 1921, Accrington were founder members of the League in 1888 and resigned in 1893 after being relegated to the Second Division.

The clubs first met on 22 December 1888 at Pikes Lane with Wanderers winning 4–1, courtesy of a David Weir hat-trick. They completed the 'double' in that inaugural season of the Football League, winning 3–2 at Accrington in what was the final game of the campaign.

The following season, Accrington gained revenge, winning 3–1 at home and 4–2 at Pikes Lane.

In 1890–91, Accrington won 2–1 at home and 5–1 in the F.A. Cup, but at Pikes Lane it was a different story with Wanderers winning 6–1, Barbour hitting a hat-trick.

The two clubs last met on 4 March 1893, Wanderers winning 5–2 and David Weir finishing as he had started with a hat-trick against the East Lancashire opposition, who are the only founder members of the League no longer in membership.

Age

Youngest: The youngest player to appear in a first-class fixture for Bolton Wanderers F.C. is Ray Parry, who played in the First Division match against Wolverhampton Wanderers on 13 October 1951, when he was 15 years 267 days old.

Oldest: The oldest player to line up in a Wanderers first team is Ted Vizard. Ted was born in Cogan, Cardiff in June 1889, so he was forty-one years old when he played his last game for us at Sunderland on 21 March 1931.

In the post-war era, Phil Neal was the most senior man to appear for the Wanderers in a first-class fixture, for he was approaching his 39th birthday when he last turned out in the 1–0 home victory over Aldershot on 22 April 1989. Tony Dunne had turned out at thirty-

Ray Parry—the youngest player to appear in a first-class fixture for the Wanderers.

seven years of age, when his career ended after a 4–1 defeat at home to Liverpool on 1 May 1979.

Goalkeeper: It seems certain that Stan Hanson is our oldest serving goalkeeper, for he was in his 40th year when he left the Wanderers in January 1956.

Aldershot

In March 1992 the liquidator who had been called in to supervise the winding up of the 'Shots' confirmed to the Football League that no offers had been received for the Fourth Division club. The two clubs first met in the Second Round of the Football League Cup on 22 September 1965 when goals from Francis Lee (2) and Wyn Davies saw Wanderers win 3–0.

At the end of the 1986–87 season, Bolton finished in a relegation play-off position. Aldershot won the two-legged tie (2–2 at Burnden and 1–0 at the Recreation Ground) to send the Wanderers into the Fourth Division for the first time in their history. The clubs last met in 1988–89 when the Wanderers did the 'double' winning 3–0 away and 1–0 at Burnden, where a Robbie Savage goal separated the teams.

Stan Anderson

In his playing days, Stan Anderson made over 500 League appearances as a wing-half for Sunderland, Newcastle and Middlesbrough and was capped twice by England.

Between 1965 and 1970, he was in charge at Ayresome Park, leading Middlesbrough out of the Third Division and then spent a year in charge of Greek side A.E.K. Athens. He had a short spell as assistant-manager at Queen's Park Rangers before joining Doncaster Rovers, where he was manager for four years before joining the Wanderers as assistant to Ian Greaves.

After the dismissal of Greaves in January 1980, Anderson took over as caretaker manager, and despite Bolton failing to win a game during that period, his position was made official at the end of the following month. However, his first game in full charge was a boost, as the Wanderers recorded only their second success of the season in defeating European cup holders, Notts Forest, courtesy of a Neil Whatmore goal.

The inevitable happened and at the end of the 1979–80 season the club were relegated from Division One. However, much was expected the following season, as Anderson had been allowed to strengthen the squad. Unfortunately, the results failed to improve and he was put under increasing pressure when there was speculation about his position.

In March 1981 George Mulhall returned to Burnden Park as Anderson's assistant. It was his return that coincided with a run to safety as in May 1981, Anderson was sacked with two years of his contract still to run.

Bolton's full league record under Stan Anderson is:

P	W	D	L	F	A
57	18	15	24	81	91

Anglo-Scottish Cup

The Wanderers entered this competition for four consecutive seasons between 1976–77 and 1979–80.

The qualifying stages took part during the pre-season on a league basis with the qualifying clubs going through to face Scottish opposition on a two-legged basis.

In 1976 the Wanderers qualified to face Partick Thistle in the knockout stages. The game at Burnden ended goal-less and the tie was settled by a disputed Alan Hansen goal six minutes from time in the game at Firhill.

In 1977 and 1978, Bolton failed to qualify for the knockout stages, but did so in 1979 to face St Mirren. The Wanderers never recovered from the opening thirty minutes of the game at Love Street. They were four goals down after twenty-five minutes and then Len Cantello who had been previously booked, was sent off.

Frank Worthington pulled a goal back just before half-time and then Taddy Nowak hit a second in the 73rd minute to give the Wanderers some hope for the second leg.

In the second leg at Burnden, the Wanderers hit back to level the scores thanks to two Sam Allardyce goals, but just two minutes from the end of extra-time, Jim Bone netted for St Mirren to put the Wanderers out of the cup on a 5–4 aggregate.

Appearances

The players with the highest number of appearances for Bolton Wanderers F.C. are as follows:

	Football League	F.A. and Football League Cups	Total
Eddie Hopkinson	519	59	578
Roy Greaves	487 (8)	80	567 (8)
Alex Finney	483	47	530
Warwick Rimmer	462 (7)	59	521 (7)
Bryan Edwards	482	36	518
Ted Vizard	467	45	512
Nat Lofthouse	452	51	503
Paul Jones	441 (4)	61	502 (4)
Roy Hartle	446 (1)	52	498 (1)
Joe Smith	449	43	492

Consecutive Appearances: Two players have made over one hundred consecutive League appearances immediately following their debuts for the club:

Jim McDonagh, 161: debut 2 October 1976 *v.* Blackpool (Home) 0–3

Phil Brown, 134: debut 27 August 1988 *v.* Southend United (Away) 0–2

Ten players have made over one hundred consecutive appearances at any time during their careers with Bolton Wanderers:

Archie Freebairn, 136: from 6 October 1894 to 21 January 1899

Bryan Edwards, 133: from 13 November 1954 to 26 December 1957

Barry Siddall, 133: from 25 August 1973 to 25 September 1976

Warwick Rimmer, 131: from 20 March 1964 to 22 April 1967

Mike Walsh, 125: from 31 December 1977 to 6 December 1980

Peter Reid, 118: from 21 December 1974 to 29 October 1977

George T. Taylor, 117: from 23 December 1933 to 3 October 1936

David Felgate, 114: from 7 February 1987 to 13 May 1989

Eddie Hopkinson, 112: from 20 August 1960 to 29 March 1963

Harry Goslin, 101: from 25 November 1933 to 14 March 1936

Jimmy Armfield

Given the opportunity to revive the Wanderer's fortunes in what was his first managerial appointment, Jimmy Armfield's playing pedigree was without question.

Acknowledged as one of the game's first overlapping full-backs, there is no doubt that his early days as a winger gave him a taste for the attacking aspect of his game. After playing for the Football League XI and England Under–23s, he made his full debut in unusual circumstances. Just hours after playing for the Under–23s in a 3–0 win in Italy, he and Jimmy Greaves were flown straight out to Rio de Janeiro. His debut in 1959 was in front of 175,000 volatile South Americans. Armfield was at left-back and up against the flying Julinho—England losing 2–0 to the World Cup holders.

Following his display in the World Cup competition in Chile in 1962, this brilliant and stylish player was voted the best right-back in the world.

After nineteen years with Blackpool and playing in a club record of 568 League games for the Seasiders, he went into management with Bolton Wanderers.

Appointed on 19 May 1971, he immediately set about restoring confidence.

The colours reverted from the all white to the traditional white shirts and navy-blue shorts. By the end of his first season in charge, he had transformed things so much, that only forty-one goals were conceded—the club's best defensive record since 1925.

The foundations had been laid and the benefits reaped in 1972–73 when Bolton secured the Third Division championship. Although numerous offers came from top clubs, Armfield stood firm as more Bolton youngsters were blooded, along with some shrewd signings in Peter Thompson and Tony Dunne.

In September 1974 Armfield finally gave way to an offer from Leeds United. He took the Yorkshire side to the 1975 European Cup Final, leaving three years later to become a full-time journalist.

He left Burnden Park in the knowledge that he had lifted the Wanderers out of their darkest hour and into a new and exciting period of their history.

Bolton's full league record under Jimmy Armfield is:

P	W	D	L	F	A
142	59	41	42	175	129

Attendances: at Burnden Park

Individual Matches: Highest The following attendances in excess of 50,000 were recorded at Burnden Park.

Opponents	Date	Competition	Attendance
Manchester City	18 February 1933	F.A. Cup Rd 5	69,912
Blackburn Rovers	6 March 1929	F.A. Cup Rd 6(R)	65,295
Manchester City	20 February 1937	F.A. Cup Rd 5	60,979
Preston North End	14 February 1959	F.A. Cup Rd 5	58,692
Liverpool	20 February 1965	F.A. Cup Rd 5	57,207
Stoke City	15 February 1958	F.A. Cup Rd 5	56,667
Wolverhampton Wanderers	1 March 1958	F.A. Cup Rd 6	56,306
Manchester United	1 September 1951	F.L. Division 1	55,477
Everton	15 October 1938	F.L. Division 1	54,564
Everton	27 February 1907	F.A. Cup Rd 3(R)	54,470
Portsmouth	20 February 1954	F.A. Cup Rd 5	53,883
Sheffield Weds	17 March 1954	F.A. Cup Rd 6(R)	52,568
Portsmouth	3 March 1934	F.A. Cup Rd 6	52,181
Manchester United	11 September 1954	F.L. Division 1	50,708
Swindon Town	31 January 1914	F.A. Cup Rd 2	50,558
Everton	15 February 1977	F.L. Cup Semi-Final	50,413

Lowest: On three occasions attendances of fewer than 3,000 were recorded at Wanderers matches at Burnden Park:

Rochdale	10 December 1991	Autoglass Cup (Q)	1,507
Chester City	30 August 1983	F.L. Cup Rd 1	2,665
Darlington	5 November 1985	F.L. Division 3	2,902

Wanderers' lowest Second Division gate at Burnden Park is 4,636 against Cambridge United on 23 April 1983, whilst the lowest crowd in their only season in the Fourth Division was 3,701 against Wrexham on 19 December 1987.

Wanderers lowest First Division gate at Burnden Park was against Portsmouth on 22 February 1933, when a crowd of 3,101 was recorded. The lowest post-war crowd for a First Division match is 4,280 against Leeds United on 3 February 1947.

Bolton Wanderers' average home league attendances over the last ten seasons have been as follows:

Division 3	1984–85	4,951	Division 3	1989–90	7,292
Division 3	1985–86	4,847	Division 3	1990–91	7,277
Division 3	1986–87	4,855	Division 3	1991–92	6,015
Division 4	1987–88	4,997	Division 3	1992–93	9,062
Division 3	1988–89	5,531	Division 1	1993–94	11,498

The lowest attendance for an F.A. Cup replay this century was 20,470 at Bolton in 1901 when Spurs beat Sheffield United 3–1. This was due largely to the railway's refusal to allow cheap excursion tickets to Bolton, where the station was being rebuilt.

Autoglass Trophy

The Autoglass Trophy replaced the Leyland DAF Cup for the 1991–92 season.

It was an injury-hit Bolton side that went down 2–1 to Preston North End on the plastic Deepdale pitch. Both North End's goals came from former Wanderers, John Thomas and Warren Joyce, with David Reeves replying for Bolton three minutes from time. Bolton qualified for the knockout stages of the Trophy when they defeated Rochdale 4–1 on a cold night at Burnden. After a goal-less first half, David Reeves hit a hat-trick inside eleven minutes. It was the second hat-trick of Reeves' career, the other coming when he was on loan at Scunthorpe who were up against Hereford, ex-Bolton goalkeeper Kevin Rose being the 'keeper that he faced on both occasions.

Andy Walker made his full Bolton debut in the Autoglass Trophy first round tie at Crewe, but it was a disappointing performance by Bolton, who crashed out of the competition to goals from Rob Edwards and Craig Hignett.

In 1992–93 the Wanderers visited Rochdale for a preliminary tie, a poor game being best remembered for the torrential downpour that lasted throughout. Keith Branagan saved a last minute penalty to make sure the game ended scoreless. John McGinlay scored Wanderers equaliser in a 1–1 draw against Bury. Visiting Darlington in the first round, Bolton found themselves well on top before hanging on late in the game. The Wanderers qualified for the next round with a 4–3

scoreline after extra-time. The club's hopes of progressing in the competition were shattered in the next round when bottom of the Second Division Huddersfield Town beat the Wanderers 3–0.

Away

Opponents	Date	Competition	Score
	Best away wins		
26 December 1914	Aston Villa	F.L. Division 1	7–1
26 December 1899	Barnsley	F.L. Division 2	6–1
23 January 1928	Blackburn Rovers	F.L. Division 1	6–1
7 April 1920	Aston Villa	F.L. Division 1	6–3
	Worst away defeats		
1 March 1890	Burnley	F.L. Division 1	0–7
1 March 1915	Sheffield Wednesday	F.L. Division 1	0–7
21 March 1936	Manchester City	F.L. Division 1	0–7
21 December 1889	Blackburn Rovers	F.L. Division 1	1–7
26 December 1902	Sheffield United	F.L. Division 1	1–7
5 September 1931	Sheffield Wednesday	F.L. Division 1	1–7
1 May 1982	Queen's Park Rangers	F.L. Division 2	1–7
8 December 1900	West Brom Albion	F.L. Division 1	2–7
10 September 1930	Liverpool	F.L. Division 1	2–7
7 December 1935	Sunderland	F.L. Division 1	2–7
18 January 1958	Manchester United	F.L. Division 1	2–7
4 September 1969	West Ham	F.L. Cup Rd 2	2–7
	Highest scoring away draws		
8 December 1888	Blackburn Rovers	F.L. Division 1	4–4
9 December 1905	Middlesbrough	F.L. Division 1	4–4
26 March 1927	West Ham	F.L. Division 1	4–4
23 February 1929	Portsmouth	F.L. Division 1	4–4

| 18 March 1980 | West Brom Albion | F.L. Division 1 | 4–4 |
| 4 September 1984 | Oldham Athletic | F.L. Cup Rd 1 | 4–4 aet |

Most Away Wins in a Season: 12 in 1904–05 (Division 2)

Fewest Away Wins in a Season: 0 in 1949–50 (Division 1) and 1979–80 (Division 1)

Most Away Defeats in a Season: 18 in 1984–85 (Division 3)

Fewest Away Defeats in a Season: 3 in 1899–1900 (Division 2) and 1904–05 (Division 2)

Most Away Goals in a Season: 37 in 1919–20 (Division 1)

Fewest Away Goals in a Season: 10 in 1897–98 (Division 1)

Best Starts

The Wanderers have been unbeaten for the first seven games of a season on three occasions: 1896–97, 1906–07, and 1934–35, when they had seven straight wins, scoring twenty-one goals and conceding two, before they lost 6–2 at Sheffield United!

Blackburn Rovers

There are some particularly vivid memories of past encounters between Wanderers and their rivals, Blackburn Rovers. The two clubs were both among the original members of the Football League and met for the first time on 8 December 1888, drawing 4–4 at Blackburn. On 7 January 1928, the Wanderers beat Rovers 6–1 at Ewood—the season that Blackburn won the F.A. Cup.

It was an unusual match in many ways. Gibson and Jack scored in the first half to put Wanderers 2–0 up, but the home side had lost both

full-backs, Hutton and Jónes, through injury. In the second half both returned, Jones at outside left and Hutton in goal as Rovers' goalkeeper Cope hurt his shoulder in making a save. Joe Smith scored two further goals and then Jack scored from a twice-taken penalty. In the closing minutes Butler got Bolton's sixth goal with Mitchell netting a consolation for Rovers.

One of the best remembered clashes between Wanders and Rovers is the F.A. Cup semi-final of 1957–58 at Maine Road. For twenty minutes or so, Blackburn looked set for Wembley and Peter Dobing put the Rovers in the lead, but defensive slips allowed Ralph Gubbins to score twice in a matter of minutes.

There was another occasion when the Wanderers beat the Rovers in the Cup and went on to lift the trophy; in fact, they took it from Blackburn. In 1929 they beat Rovers in a Burnden replay after the first meeting had set up an Ewood attendance record of 61,783. Of importance to both sides, if for different reasons, was the Second Division clash at Burnden Park on 23 March 1976, when Rovers were fighting for survival and Wanderers had high hopes of promotion. In the event, the only goal of the game, scored by John Waddington, helped save Blackburn from relegation, while it was to prove a fatal blow to Bolton's hopes of returning to the top flight.

The Wanderers gained some consolation of 27 April 1978 when their 1–0 win at Ewood with Frank Worthington getting the goal, ensured their promotion to the First Division.

Bradford Park Avenue

Park Avenue enjoyed forty-seven seasons in the League before failing to hold on to their place in 1969–70 after three consecutive seasons at the bottom of the league.

They started their career in the Second Division in 1908–09 and in 1914 joined their Bradford neighbours, City in the First Division. The clubs first met in the Yorkshire sides inaugural season in the Football league when Park Avenue won 1–0 at Burnden Park. Goals from Greenhalgh and Holden saw Wanderers win the return match in Bradford 2–1.

They were relegated in 1920–21 and the following season suffered the embarrassment of dropping into the Third Division (North). They returned to the Second Division in 1928 and it wasn't until 1950–51 that they were next relegated.

The last time the two sides met was on 30 March 1935 when Bradford won 2–1 at Burnden with G. T. Taylor getting the Wanderers goal.

Founder members of the Fourth Division, Bradford won promotion just once more before their eventual demise.

Brothers

There have been four instances of brothers playing for the Wanderers.

James Turner went to Bolton in July 1888 as an outside-left, where he partnered his brother Richard in the Reserves on a number of

Tommy and Ralph Banks—Ralph made his last first-team appearance in the 1953 F. A. Cup Final, while Tommy won a winners' medal in 1958.

occasions. The two played in all three F.A. Cup matches in 1888–89 with James hitting a hat-trick in the 9–0 win over West Manchester.

Tom Buchan who joined the Wanderers from Blackpool in May 1914, played in every position apart from full-back, even turning out as emergency goalkeeper. His younger brother John also appeared for Bolton during the war.

Tommy Banks was one of the great 'hard men' of the Bolton defence of the 1950s. Opportunities in the first team were few and far between as his brother Ralph occupied one of the full-back positions. Tommy Banks was a quality full-back with his best moments at Burnden coming towards the end of his career. In 1958, he collected an F.A. Cup winner's medal and made his England debut against the Soviet Union in Moscow. Ralph was Tommy's senior by nine years. He lost his most promising years to the war and made his last first-team appearance in the 1953 F.A. Cup Final.

Julian Darby now with Coventry City represented England at schoolboy level and appeared for the Central League side as a fifteen-year-old. A versatile performer, the only shirt he failed to pull on in his Bolton career was the goalkeepers. His brother Simon also had a spell at Burnden Park in the early 1980s, but didn't progress from the Central League side.

Burnden Park

In 1895, the site of Burnden Park was miserable; one end bound by a railway and the land a stagnant mess of dumped refuse and chemicals from nearby works. A Scarborough contractor was called in to lay out the new ground, under instructions from John Norris, who specifically requested a cycling track round the pitch, just like the one laid for the King of Italy.

Burnden Park was opened on 17 August 1895 with an athletics meeting, the town's 9th Annual Athletics Festival, attended by an impressive crowd of 15,000.

On Wednesday 11 September 1895, the ground was eventually put to its proper use when Preston North End were the visitors for a benefit game for Di Jones. The corwd of 3,000 saw North End win the game with a solitary goal from David Smith.

Three days later, the first League game took place at Burnden Park with Everton as the visitors. The game was preceeded by a cycle race an hour before the kick-off, witnessed by a 10,000 crowd which grew to 15,000 by 4 p.m.—the advertised start—Bolton winning the game 3–1.

In April 1901, Burnden was chosen as the venue for the F.A. Cup final replay between Tottenham Hotspur and Sheffield United. A crowd of 50,000 had been expected but only 20,470 turned up, due to a lack of cheap railway facilities. The occasion became known as 'Pie Saturday' (see separate entry) on account of the catering miscalculations.

Burnden Park's official highest crowd was 69,912 for the visit of Manchester City in the F.A. Cup in February 1933. During the Second World War the ground was taken over, the pitch for use by the Education Authorities, the stands by the Ministry of Supply. The Burnden Stand was still full of food supplies when the event which was to stand out in the history of all football grounds occured on 9 March 1946.

The match was unusual in itself, for that season immediately after the War, it had been decided that every Cup-tie up to the Semi-finals should by two-legged. Bolton had won the first leg of this quarter-final tie at Stoke 2–0 and an estimated 85,000 squeezed into Burnden Park in the afternoon, most of whom knew little about the tragic events at the Railway End. As the game began, hundreds spilled out on to the track, but it was not until twelve minutes later that it became apparent there had been fatalities—thirty-three bodies were found and laid out on the pitch, whilst first aid was given to hundreds. Bolton felt a great deal of remorse, although the report did not blame the club specifically. After the government report in 1947, the club spent £5,500 modernising the Railway End, improving the turnstiles and gates, adding barriers and fencing off the railway line.

On 14 October 1957, Bolton's new floodlights were switched on for a friendly against Hearts. It was claimed that they possessed sufficient power to light the streets from Burnden to Blackpool. Despite the club's fall from the top flight during the 1960s, Burnden was honoured with selection for two F.A. Cup semi-finals. The post-war crowd record at Burnden came in February 1959 when 58,692 were at a fifth round F.A. Cup tie against Preston North End. Even as recently as

 Burnden Park—home of the Wanderers since 1895.

1977, the ground housed such an atttendance when 50,413 saw the League Cup semi-final second-leg against Everton.

During the summer of 1979, 4,342 seats were put on the Great Lever End Terrace and the pitch, a poor drainer despite its camber, was dug up. All manner of compressed, rotting matter was found underneath. Undersoil heating and sprinklers were installed, though at one stage it seemed inevitable that a plastic pitch would be laid on the Burnden turf. This was vetoed by the League ruling that banned all further pitches of this nature for three years.

The greatest change took place in 1986 when the 16,000 capacity Railway End Terrace was cut in half and a Normid superstore built in the north-west corner of the Embankment on the very spot that had seen the disaster.

Though there are plans to move the Wanderers base to Horwich, history should be cherished and Burnden Park has a history and many happy memories for the thousands who have passed through its doors.

Burnley

Jack Milsom who scored four goals in Bolton's 7–0 win over Burnley in January 1935.

The first league game between the Wanderers and the Clarets took place at Pikes Lane in September 1888 in what was Bolton's second league game. Burnley arrived late and when they did appear, they were wearing similar coloured jerseys as the Wanderers. Bolton made a quick change and then romped into a 3–0 lead within the first twenty-five minutes. Tait pulled one back for Burnley just before the break and then Polland and two more from Tait, who became the first player to score a hat-trick in a league game, saw them make a brilliant recovery to win 4–3. The following season saw the Wanderers win 6–3 at home, though the Football League ordered the game to be replayed due to protests over the frosted ground. The replayed game ended 2–2, but in between these games, the encounter at Burnley took place. At the time, Bolton were on a good run and in the F.A. Cup semi-finals, Burnley were anchored at the foot of the table and without a league win in seventeen games. The Wanderers crashed 7–0 to set their worst league defeat which still stands today, although it was equalled in defeats at Sheffield Wednesday in

1915 and Manchester City in 1936.

Bolton gained some revenge for this defeat by winning by the same score at Burnden in January 1935, with Jack Milsom chipping in with four goals.

The Wanderers also scored seven against Burnley at Burnden in November 1927, but on that occasion had to be happy with a 7–1 win. The goals coming from David Jack with three and Harold Blackmore with four.

One game that doesn't appear in the official Football League records took place during the war in October 1942, when Bolton ran out 7–4 winners at Burnden in a League North match, Chadwick hitting a hat-trick.

In January 1983, supporters at Burnden witnessed one of the most incredible goals scored by the Wanderers in a league game. Burnley keeper Billy O'Rourke who had the unenviable distinction of conceding seven goals on his league debut was completely outwitted by Wanderers Republic of Ireland international keeper Jim McDonagh.

He collected the ball near his own penalty spot and with the assistance of a strong wind kicked the ball into the other half of the field. The ball bounced once before flying over the despairing O'Rourke in the Burnley goal to finish in the back of the net for Wanderers third goal in a 3–0 win!

Burton United

One of the founder members of the Second Division as Burton Swifts in 1892, they merged with Burton Wanderers (after they'd left the League) to form Burton United.

They failed to gain re-election after finishing bottom of the Second Division in 1906–07 having spent all of their fifteen seasons in the league.

The two clubs first met in 1899–1900 as Bolton won 5–2 away and 5–0 at home; Laurie Bell scoring six of the Wanderers ten goals. In 1904–05, the Wanderers won 7–1 with Sam Marsh and Walter White both grabbing hat-tricks.

Bury

The games against our friends and neighbours from Bury have never been short on excitement.

The very first game between the two clubs in the League was on 7 September 1895 at Bury, where Bolton won 3–0.

In 1990–91, Bolton beat Bury over two-legs in the play-offs (1–0 at Burnden and 1–1 at Gigg Lane) and though they came under the auspices of the league, they certainly took the form of cup-tie football. In previous two-legged games between the clubs, it is Bury who have come out on top each time. In the 1986–87 league Cup, Bury won 2–1 at Gigg Lane, the second leg being scoreless. The semi-finals of the Lancashire Cup in 1947 saw Bolton win the first leg 3–1 at Burnden but go down 3–0 in the second leg.

In the F.A. Cup, Bolton and Bury have been drawn together on four occasions, with the Wanderers coming out on top each time. The first was in 1894–95 when a goal from Jim Cassidy was enough to settle the last cup tie at Pikes Lane.

In the Sherpa Van Trophy, Bury have won both encounters in 1987–88 and 1988–89, yet despite this setback, the Wanderers went on to win the trophy in that year.

The Wanderers biggest winning margin against Bury at Burnden in the League is by 4–0 which came in December 1905, thanks to two goals from Walter White and one each from Sam Marsh and Marshall McEwan. Two seasons later, Bury recorded their best result on our ground, winning 6–3 on the opening day of the season with Harold Tufnell hitting a hat-trick for the Shakers and Albert Shepherd doing likewise for Bolton.

In 1991–92, Bolton drew at Gigg Lane 1–1 and won 2–1 at Burnden—it was the first time since 1965–66 that the Wanderers have managed to avoid defeat at least once in a term that the two clubs have faced each other.

Billy Butler

One of the greatest of all Wanderers' wingers, Billy Butler had never taken part in organised football, when he joined the Royal North Lancs Regiment at nineteen years of age.

Whilst in the army, he became a centre-forward and it was from that position that he signed for his home-town club, Atherton after being demobbed.

Bolton spotted him playing for Atherton in the Bolton Combination and in April 1920, they signed him, switching him to outside right, where he was to make his mark in League football. He made his debut in a 2–0 home defeat by Chelsea in the 1921–22 season.

He won an England cap against Scotland in 1924, partnering David Jack. He was also the holder of three F.A. Cup-winners' medals in the glorious 1920s and scored the Wanderers opening goal in the 1929 F.A. Cup Final success over Portsmouth at Wembley.

When the Wanderers were relegated in 1933, he was reunited with his former team mate Joe Smith, who was in charge of Reading. He had been on the transfer list at his own request and played in 449 first-team games, scoring 74 goals.

In 1935, he took over as Reading's manager, but resigned four years later for personal reasons.

During World War Two, Butler became a P.T. Instructor in the R.A.F. and was later manager at Torquay United.

He emigrated to South Africa, where he managed Johannesburg Rangers and coached Pietermaritzburg and District F.A.

Subsequently, he was employed as a coach by the Rhodesian F.A. He died in Durban in July 1966, aged sixty-six.

John Byrom

John Byrom joined the Blackburn Rovers' groundstaff straight from school, having already played for Blackburn Schoolboys and capped by England Youth.

After only a handful of games in Rovers' Central League side, he made his first-team debut against Birmingham City in November 1961. On Boxing Day that season, he hit the first of his four hat-tricks for Blackburn against West Ham at Upton Park. In 1964–65 he scored 25 League goals in his 40 appearances including hat-tricks against Aston Villa and West Ham.

During the 1965–66 season, Blackburn tumbled towards the Second Division and Byrom struggled to find the net, but in the club's F.A. Cup run, he scored seven goals, including his third hat-trick against West Ham.

In June 1966, John Byrom signed for Bolton Wanderers in a £25,000 deal, but the best of "J.B." was not seen at Burnden until 1969. The initial idea was for Wyn "The Leap" Davies to knock the ball down for Byrom to capitalise, but within two months, Davies had joined Newcastle United.

In the 1969–70 season, Byrom started in superb style, scoring hat-tricks in the first two games of the season—Millwall and Rochdale in the League Cup, as the Wanderers won 4–1 and 6–3 respectively. He ended the season with twenty-five goals from forty-five games. The following season saw Bolton relegated to the Third Division and as Bolton's most saleable asset he was put up for sale. Fortunately for us long-suffering Bolton fans, he stayed to top the Wanderers' goal-scoring charts in 1972–73 and win a Third Division Championship medal.

On the club's return to the Second Division, he was again top scorer with twenty-four goals in forty appearances. In the F.A. Cup tie against Stoke City, he hit a hat-trick in Bolton's 3–2 win, popping up on his own goal line in the last minute to clear and salute as if he'd just scored the winning goal in an F.A. Cup Final!

He 'retired' at the end of the 1975–76 season, after playing in over 350 games for Bolton and scoring 130 goals.

Joining Blackburn for a second time in September 1976 on a free transfer, he found age and a series of injuries were against him and at the end of the season, he finally ended his career.

Captains

By 1890, Di Jones was Bolton's captain—the ideal full-back, cool, a strong tackler and able to kick with either foot, he hardly missed a game. He skippered the Bolton team to the 1894 F.A. Cup Final, where they lost 4–1 to Second Division Notts County.

Archie Freebairn was appointed captain in 1899, taking over from Di Jones, but the Glasgow-born half-back, could do little to prevent the club's relegation for the first time.

Joe Smith's greatest honour came in 1923 when he became the first F.A. Cup Final skipper to receive the trophy at Wembley. Three years later, he lifted the trophy again as David Jack's goal was enough to beat Manchester City.

Jimmy Seddon who played in 375 first-team games for the Wanderers was at the peak of his career when he captained Bolton to victory in the in the 1929 F.A. Cup Final.

One of the finest full-backs to be denied an international career, Roy Hartle captained the side on many occasions and was a member of the 1958 F.A. Cup winning team, but that was captained by Nat Lofthouse.

A nephew of former Sheffield Wednesday and England player, Ellis Rimmer, Warwick Rimmer bridged the gap between Bolton's slump of the 1960s and the long haul back to the top flight in the 1970s. A firm favourite with the fans, he captained the team that won the Third Division championship in 1973. An ever-present in that team was Roy Greaves. He was

Phil Brown—the perfect captain, leading the team by example.

a cornerstone in the side that spent the next five seasons in Division Two before pushing their way into the top flight. It was Greaves, who was by then captain, that lifted the Second Division championship aloft in 1978.

Dave Sutton joined Bolton from Huddersfield Town in July 1985 for a fee of £12,000 and in his first season he became club captain and made a Wembley appearance in the Freight Rover Trophy final. After the Wanderers were relegated to Division Four in 1987, he played his part in leading them to promotion a year later.

Mark Came was rewarded with the captaincy at the beginning of the 1988–89 season and within a matter of weeks had collected the Lancashire Cup after the Wanderers had beaten Preston North End in the final—a trophy they had not won since 1948.

Phil Brown proved the perfect captin—leading the team by example. In a season that transformed his career after nine years of foot-slogging in the Fourth Division, he lifted the Sherpa Van Trophy in May 1989.

Central League

The Central League originated in 1911 to serve primarily the clubs in the North and Midlands reserves teams. Bolton came close on a couple of occasions to winning the Central League Championship but had to wait until 1954–55 for that honour.

The club's record that season was:

P	W	D	L	F	A	Pts
42	26	7	9	70	28	59

In the early 1980s, a decision was taken to have two divisions and in 1982–83, Bolton found themselves in Division Two. However, the Wanderers bounced straight back, but lasted only one season in the top flight before returning to the Second Division and in 1986–87, had to apply for re-election!

The season of 1990–91 saw Bolton promoted to the First Division and last season they beat Sunderland 10–1. When Owen Coyle grabbed

his fourth to round off the scoring eight minutes from time, he took the Wanderers into double figures for what is understood to be the first time in the Central League.

The club's full record in the Central League is:

P	W	D	L	F	A
2902	1039	642	1215	4498	4906

Centuries

There are nine instances of individual players who have scored a hundred or more goals for the Wanderers.

Nat Lofthouse is the greatest goalscorer with 255 strikes in his Bolton career (1946–1960) while Joe Smith scored 254 goals between 1909 and 1927. Other centurions are: David Jack (144) Jack Milsom (142) Ray Westwood (127) Willie Moir (118) John Byrom (113) Harold Blackmore (111) and Neil Whatmore (107). Only Jim McDonagh (161) and Phil Brown (134) have made over a hundred consecutive appearances immediately after making their Football League debuts.

Championships

We have on three occasions won a divisional championship:

1908–9 Second Division Champions

A season that opened disastrously was transformed into one of triumph following a vigorous public protest. Bolton lost their first match at Birmingham 2–0 and a later barren spell saw the club sink into the lower regions of the table. Club shareholders delivered an ultimatum—new players had to be signed. The directors promptly sold some of their older players and with four new signings, the results began to improve. The Wanderers finished the season in fine form, losing only one of their final twelve matches. A crowd of 30,000 saw

the Wanderers beat Derby 1–0 at Burnden Park on the final day of the
season to make sure of promotion.

	P	W	D	L	F	A	Pts
Bolton Wanderers	38	24	4	10	59	28	52
Tottenham Hotspur	38	20	11	7	67	32	51
West Bromwich Albion	38	19	13	6	56	27	51

1972–73 Third Division Champions

An encouraging 3–0 home win over Bournemouth in the opening
game boosted confidence all round and although there were a few early
stutters, we hit top form by October and after that, we were never out
of the top three. We really produced our killer blow at the end though,
winning five and drawing two of our final seven games. A 3–0 home
win over York City on Easter Saturday clinched both promotion and
the championship.

	P	W	D	L	F	A	Pts
Bolton Wanderers	46	25	11	10	73	39	61
Notts County	46	23	11	12	67	47	57
Blackburn Rovers	46	20	15	11	57	47	56

1977–78 Second Division Champions

The Wanderers got off to a fine start, dropping only one point in
their opening six games and at no time during the entire season did we
drop out of the top three. The partnership of Frank Worthington and
Neil Whatmore produced a wealth of goals and after the great disappointment of missing promotion by just one point in each of the
previous two seasons, there was a grim determination to make this
third time lucky.

A 1–0 win at Ewood Park in our penultimate game guaranteed
promotion. That was virtually a "home" game for us as the majority
of the 27,835 crowd were Bolton fans. A first half goal from Frank
Worthington gave us the points we needed. We still needed at least a
point to take the championship though. The crowd for the final game
at home to Fulham was 34,110. The result a 0–0 draw, the title was
ours.

	P	W	D	L	F	A	Pts
Bolton Wanderers	42	24	10	8	63	33	58
Southampton	42	22	13	7	70	39	57
Tottenham Hotspur	42	20	16	6	83	49	56
Brighton and Hove Albion	42	22	12	8	63	38	56

Charity Shield

On 6 October 1958, the Wanderers who were the F.A. Cup holders met League Champions Wolverhampton Wanderers, in the F.A. Charity Shield match at Burnden Park.

A crowd of 15,239 saw the Trotters win 4–1 with goals from Lofthouse (2) Bannister and Hill (penalty).

Christ Church F.C.

It was in 1874 when the club that was to become Bolton Wanderers F.C. was born. The Rev. J. F. Wright, the vicar of Christ Church was taking a great interest in the new sport of football, much of which was played in and around Bolton. He invited one of his regular church goers, schoolmaster Thomas Ogden to collect sixpence from all interested players for the purpose of buying a football.

At that time, no standard set of rules had been agreed and matches were played against local teams with rules being made up almost as they went along.

Meetings were held in Christ Church School, but the vicar, who had been appointed president, refused to permit any business to be discussed unless he was present.

Eventually other members of the committee objected and, in August 1877, it was agreed to change the name of the club to Bolton Wanderers F.C. Subsequent meetings were held at the Gladstone Hotel close to Pikes Lane, though the Wanderers moved headquarters again, this time to the Brittania Hotel at the corner of Deane Road, where they remained until becoming a limited liability company in 1895.

Clean Sheet

This is the colloquial expression to describe a goalkeeper's performance when he does not concede a goal.

Only two Wanderers goalkeepers have ever had twenty or more clean sheets in a session: Dave Felgate twenty-one (twenty-two with Cup-ties) in 1987–88, while Dick Pym had twenty (twenty-one) in 1924–25.

Colours

In the *Football Field* of 24 October 1881, the Wanderers were called 'the reds'. Later that season, they wore jerseys of 'scarlet and white-quarters' which were decorated with an embroidery representing the coat of arms of the borough. In 1884–85 the Wanderers tried out a new and startling kit for the home match against Sheffield Wednesday—'a loose white shirt with red spots' this displaced the earlier salmon pink which figured in the F.A. Cup Fourth Round tie against Notts County at Trent Bridge on 19 January 1884.

In May 1886, the Wanderers sported 'lily jerseys' and in December, blue and white, while in 1890 something akin to the present scheme appears to have been favoured.

Since then, the Wanderers have in the main worn white shirts and navy shorts, though in 1969–70, they changed to an all-white kit. On his appointment as manager, Jimmy Armfield reverted back to the traditional white shirts and navy shorts. In recent years, with the advent of sponsors, the Wanderers have sported a variety of light blue, yellow and white shirts—probably the most popular strips at Burnden Park, until the arrival of the Wanderers away strip of red and blue stripes.

Consecutive Home Games

The Wanderers played an extraordinary intense sequence of five home games in succession during just sixteen days (25 December to 9 January) in 1903–4—winning four and drawing one of the Second Division fixtures. Yet in 1900–1, Burnden Park was the venue of seven consecutive Bolton matches (including F.A. Cup ties).

In recent years, Bolton have played four games at home in succession on a number of occasions—twelve days (5 to 16 February 1991) being the shortest duration.

Cricketers

The only Wanderers players who were cricketers of real note were Ken Grieves and Harry Smith.

Australian-born Ken Grieves played in 452 first-class matches for Lancashire from 1949 to 1964, scoring 20,802 runs at 33.39 and capturing 235 wickets and 28.80. He kept goal for the Wanderers making fifty first-team appearances.

Harry Smith played first-class cricket for Gloucestershire and in one Test for England *v.* West Indies in 1928. A career total of 13,330 runs shows evidence of this reliability as a batsman and 705 dismissals (441 caught and 264 stumped) from 393 matches puts him way up in a class of his own among Gloucestershire wicket-keepers. For the Wanderers, he made only eight league appearances, scoring one goal in the 1913–14 season.

Crowd Trouble

However unwelcome, crowd disturbances are far from a modern phenomenon at major football matches and there is plenty of hooliganism and disorder at nineteenth century matches. The first occasion when the Bolton crowd was involved in misbehaviour was back in 1883, when referee Sam Ormerod was booed from the field at Pikes Lane and then assaulted at the railway station. It was recommended that the Wanderers be expelled from the Lancashire F.A. for failing to protect him, but the Football Association decided not to take any action. The Pikes Lane Ground became a very uncomfortable place for visitors and referees alike, who were greeted with 'hooting' and criticism.

Behaviour at Burnden Park though, has usually been of a high standard!

Darwen

Darwen joined the League when it was extended to fourteen clubs in 1891–92. Bolton did the 'double' over them that season (1–0 and 2–1) as the newcomers conceded 112 goals in twenty-six games to find themselves in the new Second Division.

They won promotion at the first attempt, but the Wanderers again won both matches (1–0 and 3–1) as Darwen were again relegated. They stayed in the Second Division until 1898–99 when they finished bottom of the table and conceded a league record 141 goals. They failed to gain re-election.

Death

Di Jones, as he was known, skippered the Bolton team that reached the 1894 F.A. Cup Final and in September 1895, he was awarded a benefit against Preston in the first football match to be played at Burnden Park. After leaving Bolton in 1898 to join Manchester City, he helped them to the Second Division title the following year. In August 1902, he gashed a knee in a practice game and contracted tetanus. Within eleven days he was dead.

Harry Goslin was a player whose name is written large in Bolton's history for his style, gentlemanly conduct and untimely death. He was a most popular captain who had inspired the Wanderers' staff to join the Territorial Army in 1939. He had since led a group of them in France, Africa and Italy. He was wounded in action whilst with the 8th Army Central Mediterranean Forces and died on 18 December 1943.

Harry Goslin, who was wounded in action whilst with the 8th Army and died on 18 December 1943.

Debuts

James Turner remains Bolton's only player to have scored a hattrick on his first-team playing debut for the club (*v.* West Manchester at home, 9–0 in a second round F.A. Cup tie on 10 November 1888). He had been selected for the previous rounds match away at Hurst, but the Wanderers opponents scratched from the competition.

A considerable number of Bolton players have made goalscoring debuts, the latest being Andy Walker when he came on as substitute at Exeter to score in the 2–2 draw on 11 January 1992.

Debut Double

Nine Bolton players have scored twice upon their debut, the first being James Munro in the 4–2 home win over Notts County on 6 September 1890 and the latest, Neil Whatmore in Wanderers' 3–2 win over Swansea at the Vetch Field on 4 April 1973.

Defeats

Individual Games

Bolton's worst home defeat in a first-class match was the 6–0 scoreline inflicted by Chelsea in a Fourth Round League Cup replay at Burnden Park on 8 November 1971. In the Football League, the Wanderers lost 6–2 to Preston North End on 12 October 1889, 6–3 to Bury on the opening day of the 1907–08 season and 6–4 to Arsenal on Christmas Day 1952. Away from home, the Wanderers heaviest defeat has been 7–0 which had been inflicted on the club three times: *v.* Burnley 1889–90; Sheffield Wednesday 1914–15 and Manchester City 1935–36, all in the First Division.

Over a Single Season

Bolton's worst defensive record in terms of defeats suffered in a single season was in 1970–71 when they lost twenty-five out of forty-two Second Division matches. Conversely, they only lost four Second Division games in 1899–1900 when gaining promotion to Division One.

Consecutive League matches without defeat

Bolton's best run of League games without defeat is twenty-three and was established largely in the autumn of 1990 as they amassed eighty-three points to finish in the play-offs. The run began on 13 October 1990 with a 2–2 draw at Gigg Lane against Bury and finished with a home victory over Fulham, 3–0 on 9 March 1991.

Defensive Records

Bolton Wanderers best defensive record was established in 1899–1900 and helped the club gain promotion to the First Division. The Trotters conceded just twenty-five goals in that campaign and were beaten in only four matches.

The Wanderers worst defensive record was in 1932–33 when they let in ninety-two goals and were relegated to the Second Division.

Disaster

It was on the afternoon of 9 March 1946 that Burnden Park became the scene of one of the worst disasters the English game has known, yet though thirty-three people were killed, many people present at the game were unaware of the tragedy. An estimated 85,000 crowd had poured into Burnden park—the official 'gate' figure is only 65,419—for the second leg of an F.A. Cup sixth round tie against Stoke City.

The crowd was so tightly packed that many spectators tried to get out of the ground. As the pressure mounted, two crash barriers collapsed. Spectators were hurtled forward and many were trampled underfoot. Dead and wounded were laid out on the running track, doctors being summoned from the crowd to attend to them. The game was just twelve minutes old when the referee was informed of the full extent of the disaster. He took the players off the field, but after

 Burnden Park on 9 March 1946—the scene of one of the worst disasters the English game has ever known.

consultation with the police, play was resumed after a twelve minute break. It was felt that this was the wisest decision. Play continued until its finish with no interval being taken.

In addition to the thirty-three fatalities, 500 were injured, twenty-four of whom were taken to hospital.

The Mayor of Bolton opened a Relief Fund and total of almost £40,000 was raised.

The match itself ended in a 0–0 draw, so Bolton having won the first leg 2–0, went through to the semi-finals.

Dismissals

The first Bolton player since the war to be sent off in a league match.

Although sendings–off are an all-too-common feature of the modern game, no-one should think that football has ever been immune from them.

On 18 January 1902, James Sutcliffe became the first Wanderer to be sent off at Burnden Park. During a 3–1 win over Sheffield Wednesday he was given his marching orders for bad language directed at the referee after the official allowed a goal that Sutcliffe claimed did not cross the goal line. He was later suspended for fourteen days.

John Higgins, the son of a Buxton baker became the first Wanderer since the war to be sent off in a League game. He received his marching orders at Hillsborough and was subsequently suspended for three weeks.

George Oghani's discplinary record began to catch up with him when he was sent off twice in the first half of the 1985–86 season and missed a number of games through suspension.

Draws

Bolton played their greatest number of drawn League matches in a single season (16) in 1971–72 and 1986–87 when they were relegated to the Fourth Division for the first time in their history, and their fewest (1) in seasons 1889–90 and 1890–91. Our highest scoring draw was a 5–5 thriller against Chelsea on a mud-bath of a pitch at Burnden Park on 30 October 1937. There have also been seven matches in which the Wanderers have drawn 4–4. The greatest number of drawn matches in a single Bolton cup-tie is three: the Third Round League cup-tie with Swindon Town in 1989 went to a third replay after three exciting drawn games. Unfortunately, the Wanderers went down 2–1 in the fourth encounter.

Ever Presents

There have been sixty two Bolton Wanderers players who have been ever-present throughout a Football League season. The greatest number of ever-present seasons by Wanderers' player is five, the record being held by Alex Paton and Eddie Hopkinson.
    The full list is:

No. of Seasons	Players
5	E. Hopkinson, A. Paton
4	J. McDonagh
3	B. Edwards, D. Felgate, A. Freebairn, S. Hanson, D. Holden, P. Jones, W. Rimmer, B. Siddall
2	J. Ball, P. Brown, H. A. Goslin, D. Jones, J. McNee, P. Reid, D. Stokes, J. W. Sutcliffe, G. T. Taylor, M. Walsh

No. of Seasons	Players
1	T. Barber, H. Baverstock, J. Boyd, K. Branagan, J. Brogan, T. Buchan, J. Cassidy, J. Chandler, J. Darby, J. K. Davenport, J. H. Edmondson, S. Farnworth, S. Farrimond, A. Finney, H. Gardiner, G. Gibson, R. Greaves, J. L. Hamlett, A. Hartford, R. Haworth, J. Higgins, D. Howe, D. Jack, R. Jones, J. Milne, W. Moir, J. H. Picken, D. Pym, F. Roberts, R. Roberts, J. Smith, R. Smith, J. Somerville, G. Taylor; T. Vizard, D. Weir, N. Whatmore, W. White, F. Worthington, C. Wright, J. Wright

Father and Son

There have been two instances of both father and son representing the Wanderers.

Bob Jack made his debut for the club as a replacement for Jim Cassidy in a 2–1 win at Small Heath in September 1895. He could have little realised the influence that he and his three sons David, Rollo and Donald were to have on Bolton Wanderers. Rollo joined the club from Plymouth Argyle in 1923 and stayed until 1929 whilst Donald's appearances were restricted to the Reserves. It was David Jack who is famous for scoring the first goal in a Wembley Cup Final, that made the biggest impression in Bolton colours. He was the club's top league scorer in five seasons and ended his Bolton days with 144 goals in his 295 league appearances.

Jocky Wright was signed from Clyde in June 1895 and was an ever-present in the Wanderers' first season at Burnden Park. His son Billy Wright was born in Sheffield, whilst his father was temporarily out of service with the Wanderers. He went into the Bolton team at the same time as another second generation Wanderer, David Jack. His breakthrough appeared to have come in the final game of the 1926–27 season when he hit a hat-trick in a 4–0 win over Huddersfield Town, but this wasn't the case and his 154 appearances for the club were spread over eleven seasons.

Alex Finney

Alex Finney was formerly a barber's lather-boy and later worked down the pit whilst playing for Sutton Juniors in his home town of St Helens.

After turning out for Peasley Cross and South Liverpool, he joined New Brighton and it was whilst playing for the Rakers in the Lancashire Junior Cup Final against Chorley at Burnden Park in 1922 that he was noticed by the Wanderers. New Brighton unaccountably forgot to place the left-back's name on their retained list and Bolton lost no time in signing him. He made his league debut at Birmingham in September 1922, and quickly formed an understanding with his partner at right-back, Bob Haworth.

Alex Finney was the mainstay of the Bolton defence that kept the Hammers at bay in the 1923 F.A. Cup Final, when at the age of twenty-two, he was the youngest member of the side. In 1923–24, he was the only ever-present in the Wanderers side as they finished fourth in Division One.

A cartilage operation cost Finney his place in the 1926 F.A. Cup-winning team, but he was back for Bolton's 2–0 win over Portsmouth at Wembley, three years later.

He netted the first of his two Bolton goals on 17 December 1927 from a fifty-yard free-kick in a 3–1 home win over Aston Villa.

In 1928, Finney played for the Football league when they beat the Irish League 9–1 at Newcastle. He played the last of his 530 first-team games for the Wanderers on New Years' Day 1937, the last player on Bolton's books to have played in the famous Cup Finals of the 1920s.

In August 1937, he joined Darwen, where he spent a couple of seasons before assisting Jack Atkinson at New Brighton. Living in Wallasey, he worked for the Parks Department until his retirement. He died in May 1982, aged eighty-one, with only Dick Pym from the 1923 Cup team outliving him.

First Division

Bolton Wanderers were in the First Division from the 1888–89 season until the end of the 1898–99 season when they were relegated.

The first match on 8 September 1888 saw the Wanderers entertain Derby County. Bolton's first international player, Kenny Davenport, had the distinction of scoring the club's first league goal after only two minutes play. He scored again and a goal from James Brogan gave Bolton a three-goal lead after only five minutes! Unfortunately, Derby came back to lead at half-time and won 6–3.

The club only spent one season in the Second Division before returning to the First for the next three. In fact, from 1900 to 1911, the Wanderers were promoted and relegated almost every season!

From 1911–12, the club spent twenty-two years in the top flight, before relegation in 1932–33.

Bolton needed to win their final game of the campaign against Leeds United at Burnden to stand any chance of survival. They did all that could have been asked of them, winning 5–0, but all their rivals won to condemn them to the drop.

Promotion at the first attempt was missed by a solitary point, but in 1934–35, records tumbled as Wanderers returned to the top flight.

For the return to Division One, Burnden Park's capacity was increased to 70,000. The next few seasons saw Bolton prove inconsistent with relegation battles prominent. In March 1936, they equalled their worst-ever League defeat when they went down 7–0 at Manchester City.

The Wanderers had Championship ambitions during 1951–52, but after leading the way, slipped to fifth. The mid-1950s saw the club put together some creative football that once again put them in the Championship frame. In 1956–57, the Wanderers completed the 'double' over league Champions, Manchester United. The 2–0 success at Old Trafford was the first game under floodlights on that ground and was witnessed by over 60,000 people.

During the early 1960s, the Wanderers line-up went through a transitional period and results were anything but stable. The 1962–63 season proved to be a difficult one for the Wanderers in terms of hanging on to their First Division status. That season however is best

remembered for the lack of football, the game closing down between the middle of December and beginning of March, due to severe weather.

The following season saw the Wanderers relegated. The club found themselves well adrift in 21st position during March 1964 but a tremendous last-ditch attempt to avoid the drop was put together when ten points from a possible twelve were won. The Wanderers needed to win their final home game against Wolves to avoid relegation. Just when it mattered Bolton slumped to a 4–0 defeat and as Birmingham defeated Sheffield United the following day, Bolton's run of twenty-nine years in the top flight came to an end.

The Wanderers were in the promotion hunt all the following season but hit their worst spell on the run-in with only two victories in the final eight games. In 1970–71, the Wanderers were relegated to the Third Division and though they only spent two seasons there, it was 1977–78 after three seasons of hard work that Wanderers gained promotion to Division One. Alan Gowling who signed for a club record fee of £120,000 from Newcastle in the final weeks of the 1977–78 season joined Frank Worthington as the scourge of First Division defences. It was Worthington who topped the Division One scoring chart in 1979 and also hit the 'goal of the season' against Ipswich at Burnden Park. The 1979–80 season proved to be a season of disaster as relegation was confirmed with five games remaining. The Wanderers were relegated to the Third Division in 1983 and four years later slipped into the Fourth Division for the first time in their history. Thankfully promotion was soon back to the Third after only one term and in 1992–93, Bruce Rioch and Colin Todd led the club into the Endsleigh Division One for 1993–94. While automatic promotion to the Premier League was a distant pipe-dream, a place in the last six was not beyond them at one stage. The clubs's successful F.A. Cup run not helping their cause. On a more positive note was the prolific goalscoring exploits of John McGinlay who was the First Division's top marksman. Bolton's all-time record in the First Division is:

P	W	D	L	F	A
2354	883	527	944	3785	2313

First League Game

The initial matches of the new Football League (five at the outset) were played on Saturday 8 September 1888 and the Wanderers entertained Derby County.

A sun-bathed crowd of around 3,000 at Pikes Lane saw Bolton get off to a flying start. Kenny Davenport had the distinction of scoring the club's first league goal after only two minutes play. He scored again a minute later and a goal from James Brogan gave Bolton a three-goal lead. Derby slowly but surely recovered and the goals started to come, three in double-quick time halfway through the first half and a fourth almost on the stroke of half-time. Bolton were stunned. They tried to rally themselves at the start of the second period, but Derby still drove forward and scored twice more before the final whistle to earn a first League victory.

First Minute Goals

Though there have been a number of Wanderers players that have scored goals in the first minute, Andy Walker's sensational diving header after forty-seven seconds against Huddersfield Town on 15 August 1992, claimed the distinction of being the first goal of the new season when he converted a near post cross from Mark Patterson.

Floodlights

The 1957–58 season heralded a new era at Burnden Park with the installation of floodlighting. They were officially opened on 14 October 1957 when the Wanderers entertained the unbeaten Heart of Midlothian from Edinburgh before a crowd of 21,058 who witnessed a 1–1 draw. One goal being scored for Hearts by their inside-left Wardhaugh

and one for Bolton through a penalty taken by Allcock. The referee on this occasion was Jack Clough, one in a line of notable Bolton referees.

The cost of the lighting was put at £25,000 with the four pylons in each corner of the ground carrying forty-eight lights with an additional 170 lighting points provided in the stands, pay boxes, exit areas and car park. It was claimed there was enough lighting to illuminate a path from Bolton to Blackpool. The lights, which were switched on by Club Chairman, Harry Warburton, saw further renowned visitors when, during November the Russian Army side CDSA Moscow visited Burnden, the Wanderers recording their first floodlit victory 3–0 before 34,139. The floodlights were updated in 1975, whilst the whole towers and lamps were completely renewed in 1987.

Football Association Cup

Bolton Wanderers have won the F.A. Cup four times. It was in 1881–82 that the club entered the competition for the first time and were knocked out by Blackburn Rovers in the second round. In 1884, the question of professionalism came to a head and as Bolton were embroiled in the issue, they withdrew from the competition. The F.A. decreed that a professional player could only compete in the F.A. Cup if he had been born within a six-mile radius of the club's headquarters or ground or had lived in that area for at least two years. This had repercussions on the Wanderers for after beating Eagley and Rawtenstall with weakened teams, they were drawn to meet Preston North End. Both clubs fielded ineligible players and were disqualified from the competition.

The F.A. Cup became farcical with clubs spying on their opponents players!

In 1889–90, Bolton reached the semi-finals of the F.A. Cup, losing to Sheffield Wednesday at Perry Barr, this after registering their best-ever win 13–0 over luckless Sheffield United. Jimmy Cassidy scored five, Weir four and Brogan three; Robinson claimed the other goal.

Reebok

**F.A. CUP
1st ROUND**

**GRETNA
V
BOLTON
WANDERERS**

Saturday
13th November 1993
Burnden Park, Bolton

Kick off 3.00p.m.

MATCH SPONSOR:
B. S. HEATING
B. S. GLAZING

OFFICIAL MARCHDAY MAGAZINE

GRETNA

FOOTBALL CLUB

£1.20

In 1894, the Wanderers reached the F.A. Cup final only to go down 4–1 to Second Division Notts County at Goodison Park and, incredible as it may seem, the club actually lost money by reaching the Final.

In 1903–04, after accounting for Southern League sides Reading and Southampton, the Wanderers were drawn to face formidable First Division opposition in Sheffield United at Bramall Lane. Surprisingly, Bolton swept into the semi-finals with a 2–0 win. A goal from Bob Taylor against Derby at Molineux put the Wanderers into their second F.A. Cup Final.

The Final was an all-Lancashire affair against championship chasing Manchester City, but a disputed goal by Billy Meredith took the Cup to Maine Road.

The F.A. Cup semi-finals of 1915 were reached, but Bolton were denied a Final appearance by the eventual winners, Sheffield United.

Action from the 1926 F. A. Cup Final v. Manchester City, which Bolton won 1–0.

The Bolton team line-up to be presented before the 1929 F.A. Cup Final against Portsmouth.

Burnden's record attendance was increased to 66,442 who witnessed a 3–1 F.A. Cup deafeat by Manchester City in 1922, the receipts of £5,220 at the time being the fourth largest ever in English football.

In 1923, the Wanderers were ensured a permanent place in the annals of football with a 2–0 victory over West Ham United in the first-ever F.A. Cup Final to be held at Wembley.

In 1926, David Jack, who had been the first player to score at Wembley, scored the only goal of the game against Manchester City in the Final. Bolton again secured the F.A. Cup in 1929, beating Portsmouth 2–0. Such was the confidence that by the time they reached the quarter-finals against Blackburn, the club had already received £500 worth of Wembley ticket applications. In 1932–33, the record crowd of 69,912 was attracted to Burnden Park for a fifth round F.A. Cup tie against Manchester City. The 1945–46 campaign can only be remembered for the loss of thirty-three lives on 9 March 1946, when during an F.A. Cup sixth round second-leg tie at Burnden against

BOLTON WANDERERS

OFFICIAL PROGRAMME **10p**

F.A. CUP — FIFTH ROUND

NEWCASTLE UNITED

Saturday, 14th February, 1976   Kick-off 3-0 p.m.

BURNDEN PARK

Stoke City, barriers collapsed causing not only death, but injury to many.

In 1953, Bolton gained recognition in what became known as the 'Matthews Final' when Blackpool ran-out 4–3 winners. The Wanderers had led 3–1 with twenty minutes remaining!

Back at Wembley in 1958, the Wanderers took on a decimated Manchester United side in the Final. Nat Lofthouse became the Wanderers' Cup-winner with both goals in a 2–0 win, the second of which became a major talking point, when he charged both the ball and United's 'keeper Harry Gregg over the goal-line. It wasn't until 1992–93 that F.A. Cup fever returned to the town. Having accounted for Sutton Coldfield and Rochdale in the opening rounds of the competition, the club finally drew out the F.A. Cup holders Liverpool at Burnden Park. Record receipts of £150,860 were taken and it needed a late goal from the holders to force a replay after the Wanderers had held a two–goal half-time advantage. The replay at Anfield saw the Wanderers gain national recognition for the way they outplayed and outfought the home side. John McGinlay headed home the opening goal from a David Lee cross after only three minutes and McGinlay

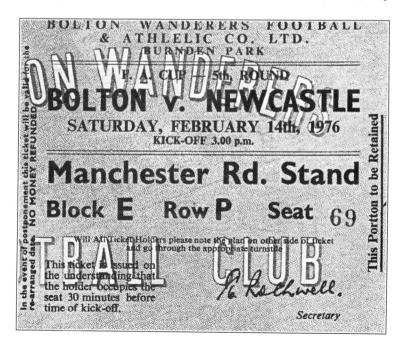

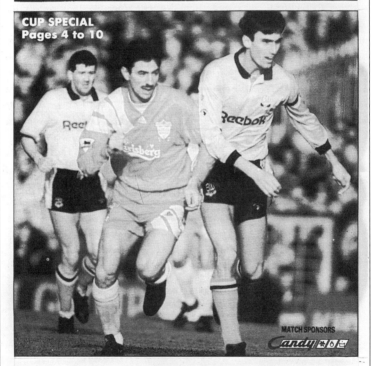

LIVERPOOL

HOLDERS OF THE FA CUP

CUP SPECIAL
Pages 4 to 10

MATCH SPONSORS

CLUB SPONSORS **Carlsberg**

FA CUP 3rd-ROUND REPLAY
LIVERPOOL v BOLTON WANDERERS
Wednesday, 13th January, 1993. 7.30 pm

ANFIELD REVIEW　　　　　　　　£1.10

turned goalmaker in the 78th minute with a perfect cross for Andy Walker to score. Bolton visited Wolves for a fourth round Cup tie, that saw goals from Green and McGinlay take them into the fifth round. The Wanderers gave Derby a run for their money, but bowed out of the competition, going down 3–1.

Last season, the Wanderers almost came to grief against the minnows of Gretna, but came back to win 3–2. Lincoln was potentially a tricky tie, but the Wanderers negotiated it competently and professionally enough. The Wanderers then drew 1–1 at home to Everton, but when they completed their second successive third round raid on Merseyside winning 3–2, the world began to sit up. Owen Coyle's extra-time winner being fit to win any Cup-tie. It was Coyle again who rescued the Wanderers in the fourth round tie agianst holders Arsenal. The club scaled even greater heights in the replay at Highbury, again in overtime. John McGinlay, Jason McAteer and Andy Walker got the goals while Alan Stubbs won widespread admiration of the pundits. It was apt that it was Stubbs who should book the quarter-final date with Oldham Athletic, his 82nd minute winner being enough to defeat Aston Villa in the fifth round.

The Wanderers who were then fourth favourites at 8–1 to lift the Cup for the first time in thirty-six years went down to the only goal of the game at Burnden—a match in which the Whites dominated. That day there was a disappointment which many of the Bolton fans had never experienced.

Football Association Cup Finals

Bolton's first Final appearance was a hundred years ago in 1894 at Goodison Park, when they surprisingly lost to the Second Division outsiders, Notts County by 4–1. That day though, the Wanderers were badly hit by injuries. Ten years later, Bolton appeared in their second Final, when this time they themselves were in Division Two. The venue for the 1904 all Lancashire battle with Manchester City was

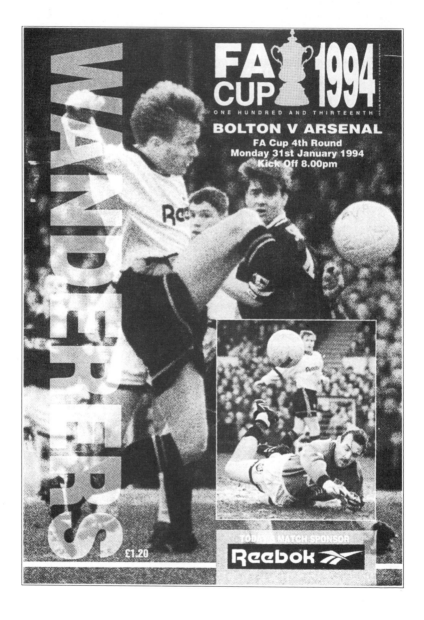

 The successful Bolton team of the 1920s.

Crystal Palace and in a rather drab affair, the legendary Billy Meredith won the Cup for City with the game's only goal.

Bolton's next Final was the memorable 1923 'White Horse Final' at Wembley against West Ham United, when an estimated 200,000 fans got in to see the Wanderers win 2–0. David Jack and Joe Smith scored the goals—that victory was the start of a great Cup era for Bolton.

For in 1926, Bolton went back to Wembley to oppose Manchester City in that season's F.A. Cup Final and only an injury to full-back Finney stopped them fielding the same side which had beaten West Ham three years previous. Bolton won 1–0 thanks to another David Jack goal and thus gained revenge for their defeat by City in the 1904 Final.

Bolton made it a hat-trick of Wembley wins in 1929 when they defeated Portsmouth 2–0. Bolton's team included Pym, Howarth, Finney, Seddon, Nuttall and Butler, all of whom collected winners' medals six years earlier. In their three Wembley visits, Bolton utilised

only seventeen players and did not concede a single goal. It wasn't until 1953 that Bolton again reached Wembley. That was the year of the 'Matthews Final' and indeed, it was Stan's brilliance late in the second half which finally broke plucky Wanderers. The 4–3 scoreline also created a new record for the competition, because never before had a side hit three goals in a Final and lost!

However, Bolton gained some consolation five years later, when they beat Manchester United 2–0 in a Final which was emotionally effected following that tragic air crash in Munich which caused the death of so many of United's top players and officials.

Nat Lofthouse.

Footballer of the Year

Only one Bolton player had been honoured by the Football Writers' Association as their choice for Footballer of the Year—England centre-forward Nat Lofthouse in 1952–53.

Football League Cup

Sad to relate, the Wanderers have failed to make much impact upon the Football League (later Milk and Littlewoods and Rumblelows and Coca Cola) Cup, with the exception of 1976–77 when they reached the semi-final only to lose over two-legs to Everton.

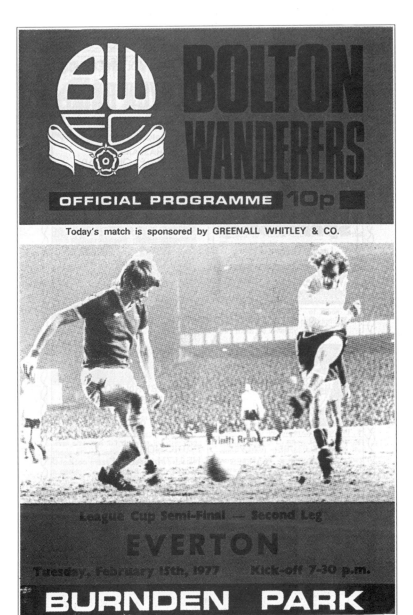

The Wanderers were then in the Second Division as they drew the first-leg at Goodison 1–1 with Neil Whatmore grabbing an equaliser with just two minutes left on the clock to send the Bolton fans home happy. The club's dreams of Wembley faded as a 23rd minute goal from Bob Latchford settled the issue. It was a disconsolent Bolton side that left the pitch, knowing they had not done themselves justice, with probably their poorest home performance of the season.

The club first took part in the competition in 1960, the initial game taking place at Boothferry Park, where the Wanderers played out a goal-less draw with Hull City. The replay at Burnden saw Bolton win 5–1 with Freddie Hill and Bill AcAdams each finding the net twice, the other goal coming from Brian Birch.

The club's best scoreline in the League Cup came in the second round of the inaugural season when Grimsby Town were defeated 6–2 at Burnden, Nat Lofthouse grabbing a hat-trick in what was his first League Cup-tie.

Few will argue that our best results were the 3–2 defeat of Liverpool in the second round replay of 27 September 1967 and the 3–0 win over Manchester City in the third round on 5 October 1971.

The Wanderers have also come in for one or two heavy defeats in the competition, namely: 7–2 at West Ham United on 4 September 1968; 6–0 at home to Chelsea in a fourth round replay on 8 November 1971 and 6–1 at Notts County on 30 October 1984. We were also involved in the longest tie in the competition when we played Swindon Town in 1989–90. It took three replays and 450 minutes in all before Swindon won 2–1.

Roy Greaves holds the record number of appearances in the competition for the club, with a total of forty-one between 1965 and 1979, whilst Tony Philliskirk heads the goalscoring chart with a total of twelve, his final goal coming in the Wanderers 1–0 win at Wimbledon in a second round second-leg tie in 1992–93. Bolton's record to date in the League Cup (correct to August 1994) is as follows:

P	W	D	L	F	A
106	37	28	41	168	188

Foreign Opponents

There have been a number of overseas visitors to Burnden down the years, the first being a South African touring team known as 'the Kaffirs' in October 1899 and they were defeated 13–3! A crowd of 1,500 witnessed what was described as a farcical game with the Wanderers running up an 8–1 half-time advantage, including a goal by 'keeper Jack Sutcliffe.

The Wanderers first overseas tour came in May 1909 with a visit to the Netherlands, where they were advertised as the Second Division champions of Great Britain. The highlights of a five game tour, which all ended in victory, were the 3–0 defeat of Dutch champions Sparta and the 10–1 success against Dordrecht. The next tour was to Germany and Austria, a seven game itinerary, producing just one defeat, that at the hands of the Victoria Berlin team by 2–1. As in previous overseas visits, the Wanderers saved the best till last, ending with a 12–0 win against the German Association in Breslau with Billy Hughes scoring five goals.

An unbeaten eight game tour to France and Switzerland, where the Wanderers were big draws after their 1923 F.A. Cup success, broke new ground. One of the games was against Young Boys of Berne who were coached by former Wanderer Jimmy Hogan.

After another cup success in 1929, the Wanderers were invited to open a new 65,000 all-seater stadium in Barcelona against the Cataluna Club. Unfortunately Bolton went down to a 4–0 defeat before the Spanish King.

It wasn't until November 1957 that Burnden Park witnessed continental visitors in the shape of CDSA Moscow. A crowd of 34,139 saw the Russian Red Army side defeated 3–1 with goals from Lofthouse, Parry (penalty) and Gubbins.

Visits to Scandinavia in the early 1950s were replaced by visits to organised tournaments and in 1958, Bolton took on Flamengo de Rio of Brazil in Paris and drew 1–1 after extra-time with Doug Holden scoring. A penalty competition ended in a 3–3 draw but the Wanderers won on the toss of a coin. Unfortunately they lost out in the final by 2–1 to Racing Club Paris.

Alitalia
OFFICIAL CARRIER

ANGLO-ITALIAN CUP
INTERNATIONAL STAGE

BOLTON WANDERERS
V
BRESCIA

Tuesday
9th November 1993

Kick off 7.30p.m.

MATCH SPONSOR:
BUTCHERS ARMS

Reebok

BOLTON Wanderers

£1.20

Having just completed a hard league season which had seen them finish fourth in the First Division, the Wanderers were invited to play ten fixtures in Rhodesia and South Africa in May and June 1959. The Wanderers were hardly prepared for such a trip, coming from the rain and mud to the baked surfaces of South Africa, but won eight and lost two of the ten games.

In March 1961, French side Le Havre AC came to Burnden in what was the second leg of an Anglo-French-Scottish Friendship Cup-tie. The two sides had drawn 1–1 in France, but Wanderers ran out 4–0 winners in the return.

The next club to come to Burnden were West German side IFC Saarbruken. Goals from Ernie Phythian (2) Dennis Stevens and Freddie Hill saw Bolton emerge as 4–1 winners.

Twelve months later, RFC Liege of Belgium came to Burnden, with Bolton keeping up their unbeaten home record against continental opposition by winning 3–2. In fact, the Wanderers first defeat on home soil came at the hands of Ajax Amsterdam in August 1979 when the Dutch side won 3–1.

Last season, the Wanderers qualified for the international stages of the Anglo-Italian Cup and though the club didn't reach the final, they were undefeated—Ancona (Home 5–0) Brescia (Home 3–3) Pisa (Away 1–1) and Ascoli (Away 1–1).

Foreign Players

The first foreign player to represent the club was Tadeus Nowak who signed from Polish side Gornik Zagreb in 1978–79. The second was Dusan Nikolic who joined the Wanderers for a reported £180,000 from Red Star Belgrade in October 1980. Other players with foreign sounding surnames include George Oghani and Peter Olinyk, the latter being Bolton born and bred!

Fourth Division

Bolton Wanderers F.C. have spent just one season in the Fourth Division, 1987–88, when we finished third and were promoted. The club had a very impressive home record of 15 wins, 6 draws and 2 defeats, though the goalscoring exploits of John Thomas with 22 league goals were the difference between success and failure.

Bolton's record in Division Four is:

P	W	D	L	F	A
46	22	12	12	66	42

Charles Foweraker

The most successful manager in Bolton Wanderers' distinguished history, Charles Foweraker, entered football in a part-time capacity in 1895, acting as a checker when Burnden Park opened, whilst employed by the old Lancashire and Yorkshire Railway Company.

After guiding the Wanderers through the majority of the war years, he was appointed secretary-manager in July 1919. He was in charge of the club throughout Bolton's most successful period, during the 1920s when the Wanderers won three F.A. Cup Finals at Wembley and were serious contenders for the First Division championship.

Foweraker became one of the most influential personalities in the development of Bolton Wanderers and was awarded the Football League's long-service medal in recognition of more than 21 years in the Wanderers' employment.

He had no experience of playing football at a high level but his success as a manager was due to his brilliant handling of players and the contacts he made over the years.

In 1933, the Wanderers were relegated, but Foweraker made a few astute signings and within two years the Trotters won promotion. In 1939 with war looming he had two teams prepared for the visit to Stamford Bridge in case a sudden call on players in the Territorial

Army decimated the chosen side. When war was declared he worked for the club on a voluntary basis until football returned and money was forthcoming.

During the war, he was a manager without a team, but despite warnings by some of the directors, he struggled and schemed to get the club re-opened in January 1941.

Foweraker strongly believed in the development of players under military age and it was from this belief rose the greatest of Bolton heroes, Nat Lofthouse.

In August 1944, Foweraker was forced to retire through ill-health, having completed 49 years' continuous service with the Wanderers. He died at his home in Bolton in July 1950 at the age of 73.

Bolton's full league record under Charles Foweraker is:

P	W	D	L	F	A
840	338	211	291	1432	1277

Freight Rover Trophy

A competition designed solely and specifically for Associate Members of the Football League, the Freight Rover Trophy replaced the initial Associate Members Cup for the 1984–85 season.

Bolton's first game in the Freight Rover Trophy was on 22 January 1985 when two goals from Warren Joyce helped the Wanderers beat Crewe Alexandra 3–2. That season, the Whites reached the Northern Area semi-final only to go down 2–1 at home to Mansfield Town.

The following season and at the end of Phil Neal's first term in charge, the Wanderers reached the Freight Rover Trophy Final at Wembley, only to lose 3–0 to Bristol City.

In 1986–87, the Wanderers rather surprisingly went out 2–1 at home to Chester City in the Northern Area quarter-final.

Gainsborough Trinity

Gainsborough Trinity spent 16 seasons all in the Second Division between 1896 and 1912 without ever managing to finish any higher than sixth.

The two clubs first met on 16 December 1899, Wanderers drawing 1–1 at Gainsborough, before winning the return 3–0. Their next meeting in season 1903–04 saw Wanderers win 5–0 at Burnden with Sam Marsh grabbing a hat-trick.

In fact, the Wanderers won all five of their home matches, scoring 20 goals and conceding just one!

Glossop North End

Glossop won promotion to the First Division at the end of their first season in the League in 1898–99. They were relegated the following season and spent the rest of the time in the lower division. They finished bottom of the table in the last season before World War One 1914–15 and resigned from the League shortly before the resumption of matches in 1919.

The first encounter between the two clubs in 1903–04 saw Glossop win 1–0, though the Wanderers won six and drew one of their other confrontations.

Goalkeepers

Bolton Wanderers F.C. has almost always been extremely well served by its goalkeepers and most of them have been highly popular with the supporters.

Eddie Hopkinson with 578 Wanderers appearances between 1956 and 1969 must be rated as the greatest goalkeepers we have ever had.

Not only did he play more than a hundred and fifty more games for the club than any other 'keeper, but won 14 full caps and an F.A. Cup winners' medal in 1958.

Dick Pym was the Wanderers goalkeeper in the famous 1923 Final. Signed from Exeter City, his qualities were soon recognised and he appeared for the Football League in Belfast. Incredibly, despite his seafaring background, he was seasick on the crossing from Liverpool!

Charlie Wright was one of the biggest characters to have been seen at Burnden Park, where he served as a player, coach and manager. Among three international appearances for Hong Kong while on National Service in the Lancashire Regiment, he played against Peru and saved a penalty in a 2–1 win.

Jim McDonagh has the unusual record of being capped for two different countries. Signed from Rotherham United, it was while he was playing for the Millers against Bolton at Burnden Park on 25 November 1972, that he thought the ball had gone out of play and placed it for a goal-kick. But Garry Jones nipped in and pushed the ball into the net for what was the winning goal, 2–1 to Bolton! Whilst in the Wanderers

Ray Westwood, who scored 127 goals for the Wanderers between 1931 and 1947.

colours, he became one of the handful of goalkeepers to score in a league game, when he netted with a huge kick downfield in January 1983 as Bolton beat Burnley 3–0.

Dave Felgate one of Wanderers' most recent 'keepers had by the end of the 1979–80 season reached a total of 61 Football League appearances without playing once in the competition for Bolton, the club which held his contract.

Goalscoring

For the Club

The Wanderer's highest goalscoring tallies were achieved in 1934–35 when the team that took the club to promotion from Division Two hit 96 league goals in 42 matches and in 1904–05 when the Trotters scored 87 goals in 34 matches to again finish as runners-up in the Second Division.

By the individual

The following players have scored 50 or more League goals for the club:

Player		Goals
Nat Lofthouse	(1946–1960)	255
Joe Smith	(1909–1927)	254
David Jack	(1921–1929)	144
Jack Milsom	(1930–1938)	142
Ray Westwood	(1931–1947)	127
Willie Moir	(1946–1955)	118
John Byrom	(1966–1976)*	113
Harold Blackmore	(1927–1932)	111

Neil Whatmore	(1973–1984)*	107
Francis Lee	(1960–1967)	92
Dennis Stevens	(1953–1962)	90
Walter White	(1902–1908)	88
Albert Shepherd	(1904–1908)	85
James Cassidy	(1889–1898)	84
Frank Roberts	(1914–1922)	79
Freddie Hill	(1958–1969)	74
Sam Marsh	(1902–1911)	72
Ray Parry	(1951–1960)	68
Wyn Davies	(1962–1966)	66
Roy Greaves	(1965–1980)	66
Billy Butler	(1922–1933)	65
Ted Vizard	(1910–1931)	64
Tony Caldwell	(1983–1987)	60
Billy Hughes	(1908–1913)	51
Tony Philliskirk	(1989–1992)	51

* Players have had two spells at Burnden Park.

All dates refer to calendar years of debuts and last appearances. Correct to August 1994.

Ian Greaves

The departure of Jimmy Armfield for Leeds United at the commencement of the 1974–75 season presented a speedy return to management for Ian Greaves who had only recently joined Bolton as assistant-manager after relinquishing his post at Huddersfield Town.

Greaves spent six years in charge at Leeds Road and in only his second season, led them back into the First Division after a long absence. But after two years and a spot of trouble with some key players who were released, the club dropped back into Division Two and later

 Bolton manager from 1974 to 1980—there were many who likened his departure to a 'death in the family'.

made a dive right down to the Fourth Division, but Greaves had left before that happened.

Ian Greaves joined Manchester United in the early 1950s and won his league debut for them in 1954–55. Being a defender, he found he had a mammoth task to displace players of the calibre of Roger Byrne, Bill Foulkes and Duncan Edwards, so his first-team opportunities were rare.

The tragic Munich air crash provided the unhappy opening for his breakthrough and later that year, he played in the F.A. Cup final against the Wanderers.

In December 1960, after 67 League appearances for United, he moved to Lincoln City, before ending his playing career with Oldham Athletic in 1962.

At Bolton, Manager of the Month awards came his way in January 1975, November 1976, August 1977 and October 1977 and in 1977–78, he was named as Second Division Manager of the Season, as the Wanderers secured the Second Division championship. He broke the club's transfer record four times before his dismissal in January 1980, with Bolton rooted at the foot of the First Division. There were many who likened his departure to a 'death in the family'.

He returned to management with Oxford United and Wolverhampton Wanderers before becoming assistant at Hereford United. In 1983 he took over at Mansfield Town, leading them to promotion and victory at Wembley in the Freight-Rover Trophy.

Bolton's full league record under Ian Greaves is:

P	W	D	L	F	A
227	90	64	73	310	274

Roy Greaves

It was a case of 'local boy made good' as Roy Greaves, born in Farnworth, spent his apprenticeship at Burnden and made his league debut in October 1965, aged 18 in a 1–0 defeat at Leyton Orient.

The following Saturday, he played at centre-forward for his first home game and scored both Bolton's goals in the 3–2 defeat by Southampton.

He then settled into the Wanderers side at inside-forward, becoming a regular in 1967, and was the club's leading goalscorer in seasons 1967–68 and 1968–69.

After relegation to the Third Division in 1970–71, Greaves was played in a much deeper position by manager Jimmy Armfield and attracted interest from both Liverpool and Arsenal.

When the Wanderers won the Third Division championship in 1973, Greaves was an ever-present and a cornerstone of the side that spent the next five years in Division Two before pushing their way into the top flight.

By then, Roy Greaves had become captain and it was he who lifted the Second Division championship trophy aloft at the end of the 1977–78 season.

In his debut season in the First Division, Greaves missed only one game, a 3–2 home defeat by Ipswich Town, but the following term, a lack of form and injuries cost him his place. His last appearance in a Bolton shirt was in an F.A. Cup defeat at Highbury in February 1980. A month later, he joined Seattle Sounders in the North American Soccer League, being just short of breaking the Wanderers' League appearance record.

After his stint in America, Greaves returned to become player-coach at Rochdale, thus giving him the distinction of having played in every division of the League.

After leaving Scotland, he continued to play in local football and is still a well-known figure in the town of Bolton, where he has business interests.

Guest Players

The 'guest' system was used by all clubs during the two Wars. Although at times it was abused almost beyond belief (in that some sides that opposed Bolton had ten or eleven 'guests'!) it normally worked sensibly and effectively, to the benefit of players, clubs and supporters alike.

The most distinguished player to 'guest' for Bolton Wanderers was Tom Finney, who in 1942, played at Turf Moor as the Wanderers beat Burnley 2–1. Bill Shankly had also promised to play for the Wanderers, but he was transferred with his unit to Scotland and played for East Fife. However, the following season, he did manage to play in two games for the Wanderers whilst on leave, scoring in the 3–0 defeat of Oldham Athletic.

During the First World War, Joe Smith and Ted Vizard 'guested' for Chelsea, whilst Jack Feebury represented Notts County. In World War Two, Norwich City had the services of Harry Goslin, Don Howe and John Roberts; Goslin and Howe also 'guested' for Chelsea and Newcastle United respectively. Jack Atkinson 'guested' for Blackpool and Everton; Alf Anderson, Rochdale; Harry Hubbick, Blackpool and Dan Murphy, Bury, whilst Matt Gillies 'guested' for three London clubs, Arsenal, Chelsea and Queen's Park Rangers. The Wanderers' life was not made any easier by other league clubs unwilling to reciprocate in the loaning of guest players. Norwich City who had the services of a number of Bolton players, failed to reply to a request to play an R.A.F. man stationed locally!

Halifax Town

The Shaymen lost their Football League status at the end of the 1992–93 season. Having played their first Football League game on 27 August 1921 in the Third Division (North), the club enjoyed sixty-five seasons without ever winning a League Championship.

The two clubs first met at Burnden Park on 29 September 1971 when a Roy Greaves goal secured a point for the Wanderers in a 1–1 draw. The following season, Stuart Lee hit a hat-trick in Bolton's 3–0 home success. The last league encounter between the two sides was at the Shay on 12 January 1988 when they played out a goalless draw.

Undefeated against the Yorkshire side in the Football League, the Wanderers were taken to three matches in the First Round of the 1986–87 F.A. Cup competition, before goals from Thompson, Caldwell and Gavin saw Bolton win the second replay 3–1.

Happy

During the 1968–69 season, Bolton supporters were invited to submit their ideas as to the name of the character above. Nat Lofthouse and club captain Dave Hatton judged the entries and came up with *Happy*.

The club shop became the *Happy* shop and there was a *Happy* Burnden Beat in full swing where record requests and messages could be sent.

During the following season, a two-foot high model in wood of the mascot was stolen from a cartoon exhibition at Smithills Coaching House—the search for *Happy* was on!

Hat-tricks

Bolton Wanderers players have netted 126 hat-tricks in Football League games with Nat Lofthouse and Joe Smith sharing the record with 9 each, closely followed by Jack Milsom on 8.

The best sequence came in October 1928 when Harold Blackmore scored three against Portsmouth and Aston Villa and George Gibson did likewise against Sheffield United all in successive weeks.

The last hat-trick hero in a League game for Wanderers was John McGinlay against Middlesbrough on 23 April 1994 as Bolton ran out winners 4–1.

 John McGinlay, seen here scoring against Blackpool, was the last Wanderers player to score a hat-trick.

In the 1970s, the Wanderers went seven years without a hat-trick hero. Stuart Lee grabbed his only hat-trick against Halifax Town at Burnden Park in April 1973 and despite the Wanderers success in winning promotion to Division One, it wasn't until August 1980 that Brian Kidd ended the spell against Newcastle United.

Since the Second World War, there have only been six hat-tricks scored by Bolton players on opposition soil in the Football League. Nat Lofthouse and Francis Lee have each hit two, Willie Moir netted four at Aston Villa in 1948 and John Thomas got three at Peterborough in January 1988.

Although twenty-one players have joined the exclusive hat-trick club since the War for Bolton, it is surprising to find the likes of John Byrom who scored 113 League goals for Wanderers, managed only one hat-trick, that coming on the opening day of the 1969–70 season. Moreover, Neil Whatmore who grabbed 107 League goals for Bolton, somehow failed to register a hat-trick for the club.

Perhaps one of the strangest hat-tricks is the fact that the Wanderers entertained Birmingham City on three consecutive New Year's Day fixtures from 1924 to 1926, winning two and drawing one!

Freddie Hill

Emerging from junior football in his home city of Sheffield, Freddie Hill signed for Bolton Wanderers in 1957. He had turned down an offer from Sheffield Wednesday in the hope of getting regular first-team football with the Trotters.

He made his League debut for the Wanderers in April 1958 at the age of 18 as a replacement for Dennis Stevens in a 1–1 draw against Newcastle United at Burnden Park.

When Nat Lofthouse had to retired due to injury, it was Dennis Stevens who replaced him at centre-forward, allowing Freddie Hill to become a permanent member of the attack at inside-forward. He had already begun to show his goalscoring ability when he netted 7 goals from his 18 appearances in 1958–59. On 4 March 1959, he hit the first of his two hat-tricks for the Wanderers in a 6–0 mauling of Chelsea on a very windy night. In the 1961–62 campagin, he netted 14 goals in 41 games—it was his best return to date.

After only three seasons in League football, his ability was recognised when he was selected for the England Under–23 side. In October 1962, he was chosen to play in his first full international against Northern Ireland in Belfast. In November of the same year, he played against Wales at Wembley, but it was his last appearance in an England shirt. The third round F.A. Cup tie against Sheffield United at Bramall Lane was played at the 13th attempt, but Wanderers lost 3–1. There was an immediate revenge however, for

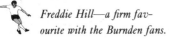

Freddie Hill—a firm fav-ourite with the Burnden fans.

Freddie Hill hit his second hat-trick to secure the points against United in Bolton's first home league game for three months.

In the two year period 1962–64, Freddie Hill asked for a move on four occasions. His last request was accepted with great regret, for Hill was a firm favourite with the Burnden fans. Liverpool were set to pay

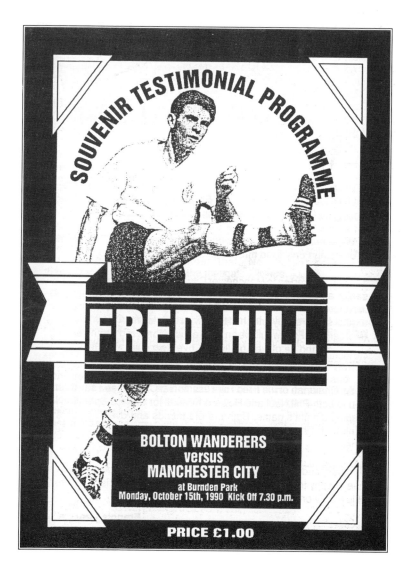

£60,000 for him, but withdrew their offer after Hill failed a medical due to high blood pressure.

The 1964–65 season was Hill's best in terms of goals, the scheming inside-forward hitting 15 goals in 41 matches. He played until the end of the 1968–69 campaign, playing in 412 games for the Wanderers and scoring 79 goals.

He left Bolton in July 1969 in a £5,000 deal for Halifax Town, but within a year, he was back in the top flight with Manchester City who paid £12,000 for Hill's services. At Maine Road, he teamed up with Francis Lee and Wyn Davies to revive old Bolton partnerships. In August 1973, he moved to Peterborough United, where he ended his League career.

In October 1990, this popular player was granted a late, but thoroughly deserved testimonial when Bolton entertained Manchester City.

Doug Holden

Doug Holden began his footballing career in his native Manchester with Princess Road School. He later joined Manchester YMCA, the Lancashire Amateur League side, for whom his three brothers all played.

Signed as an amateur for the Wanderers in 1948, he appeared for England Youth before completing his National Service. He made his league debut for the Wanderers against Liverpool in a 1–1 draw at Anfield in November 1951. He was only 17, but quickly proved that he possessed the temperament for the big occasion. He'd only made 12 appearances for the Wanderers Reserves in the Central League before his promotion to the first-team. Holden made 25 appearances that season, playing primarily on the left flank, but it was on the opposite wing that he made a name for himself, playing in the 1953 F.A. Cup Final against Blackpool in that position.

Five years later, he reverted to the left wing for the 1958 F.A. Cup Final against Manchester United—in fact, he and Lofthouse were the only two Bolton players to appear in both of those Finals.

In March 1959, he played for the Football League XI against the Irish League in Dublin. Impressing in that match, he was selected for the full England side against Scotland at Wembley.

His best goalscoring-wise was 1961–62, Holden hitting 11 goals from 32 appearances.

In November 1962, after spending 11 seasons with the Wanderers, he joined neighbours Preston North End. At Deepdale, he proved himself a worthy addition to a lengthy list of mature, ready-made players who went to Preston after earning their reputations elsewhere.

Doug Holden was one of the unluckiest of players when shooting. Often the ball somehow managed to find its way to the woodwork or else a defender miraculously got in the way. His chief asset was his ability to work well in a confined space. Often there didn't seem room to squeeze a football between the line and the full-back, but somehow Doug got through, ball as well!

After ending his League career at Deepdale, he emigrated to Australia in 1965, becoming a player-coach for Hakoah and Auburn in Sydney. He also played for the Australian national side.

In November 1970, he returned to England, having spells as trainer at Grimsby and manager of Southern League side Dartford, before leaving the game to become a car salesman.

Home Matches

Wanderers' best home wins were the 13–0 rout of Sheffield United in a Second Round F.A. Cup match on 1st February 1890 and 10–2 against Belfast Distillery in the previous round. The season before had seen the Wanderers defeat West Manchester 9–0 in the Second Round of the F.A. Cup. In 1934–35, Bolton beat Barnsley 8–0 in a Division Two game, whilst more recently, Bolton beat Walsall 8–1 on 10 September 1983 with Tony Caldwell grabbing five goals. There have also been three occasions when Bolton have won by a 7–0 scoreline: West Bromwich Albion on 7 December 1889; Loughborough Town on 30 December 1899 and Burnley on 2 January 1935.

Wanderers worst home defeat was a 6–0 hiding delivered by Chelsea in a Fourth Round League Cup replay on 8 November 1971. We have

also conceded six goals at home on three other occasions: 6–2 *v.* Preston North End in 1889–90; 6–3 *v.* Bury in 1907–08 and 6–4 *v.* Arsenal in 1952–53. There have been four occasions when we have gone down 5–0: Everton on 20 September 1890; Bristol City on 7 February 1903; Arsenal on 1st January 1937 and Blackburn Rovers on 29 February 1964.

The highest scoring home matches other than those mentioned above are a 7–3 victory over Notts County on 9 March 1889 and the 6–4 victory over Queen's Park Rangers on 29 November 1969.

Home Seasons

Bolton Wanderers have gone through a complete League season with an undefeated home record on two occasions: 1910–11 when we won 17 and drew the other two league games to gain promotion from the Second Division and 1920–21 when we won 15 games and drew the other six to finish third in the First Division.

Our highest number of home wins in a League season is 18. We achieved this number of victories in 1924–25 from a 21 match programme and in 1972–73 and 1992–93 from 23 games.

Eddie Hopkinson

Born in Wheatley Hill, County Durham, Eddie Hopkinson became a 'naturalised' Lancastrian when his family moved south to Royton near Oldham. He was soon signed as an amateur for Oldham Athletic and was only 16 years of age when he played in three Third Division North games in 1951–52.

In the summer months he played cricket for Royton in the Central Lancashire League and until football stopped him, he was a county water-polo player.

At the end of the 1951–52 season, Oldham Athletic overlooked him to Bolton's lasting satisfaction. He joined the Wanderers in August

 Eddie Hopkinson, the holder of Bolton's all-time appearance record is applauded on to the pitch by his team-mates.

1952, signing professional forms the following November. He played little football for Bolton during National Service as he was stationed in Scotland.

His meteoric rise began in August 1956 when Bolton's regular goalkeeper Ken Grieves, the Lancashire cricketer, couldn't be released from his cricketing duties as Lancashire were chasing Championship honours. Eddie got his chance in the senior side against Blackpool and went through a brilliant first season without missing a game.

At 5 ft 9½ ins he was one of the smallest goalkeepers in the First Division. In the summer of 1957, he was awarded the first of six England under-23 caps on a tour behind the Iron Curtain. In October of that year, he made his first full international appearance against Northern Ireland, going on to play against all three countries in the Home Internationals and eventually collecting 14 caps.

In 1958, he kept a clean sheet to win an F.A. Cup winners' medal as the Wanderers beat Manchester United 2–0 at Wembley.

At Norwich City in January 1969, he broke Bolton's long-standing appearance record set by Alec Finney. Eddie played in 578 matches for Bolton and but for an injury which kept him out of the side for most of the 1958–59 season and another which put him out of action for a ten-match spell in the 1963–64 season, he would have passed the Finney record much earlier.

Professionals reckon that consistency is the true test of the top-class player and there were certainly few to rival Eddie Hopkinson in this aspect of his game.

He remained Bolton's first-choice goalkeeper until the middle of the 1969–70 season when injury forced his retirement. He was awarded a testimonial in May 1971 at Burnden in a game which Portuguese World Cup stars Eusebio and Simoes appeared.

He became assistant trainer at Burnden Park, coaching both the Youth and Reserve sides. He left in July 1974 to join nearby Stockport County as assistant manager and where his son Paul kept goal.

He made an unexpected comeback when he volunteered to keep goal for the team he managed, Ashton United, when four players failed to show up for the Cheshire League game at Witton. Witton won 7–0 but 'Hoppy' got a great ovation as he retired at half-time to make way for latecomers.

In 1979 he returned to Bolton as goalkeeping coach, but eventually left the game to become a representative for a chemical company.

International Players

Wanderer's most capped player (ie: caps gained while players were registered with the club) is Nat Lofthouse with 33 caps. The following is a complete list of players who have gained full international honours while at Burnden Park.

England	caps	Wales	caps
T. Banks	6	D. Davies	3
W. Bannister	1	R.W. Davies	16

M. Barrass	3	T.P. Griffiths	4
W. Butler	1	W. Jennings	11
J.K. Davenport	2	D Jones	11
G.K. Eastham	1	E. Jones	1
H.W. Hassall	1	J. Powell	1
F. Hill	2	J.H. Roberts	1
A.D. Holden	5	R. Roberts	7
E. Hopkinson	14	J. Trainer	1
D.B.N. Jack	4	J. Vaughan	1
F.W. Kean	2	E.T. Vizard	22
R. Langton	2		
N. Lofthouse	33	*Northern Ireland*	
H. Nuttall	3	W. Hughes	1
R.A. Parry	2	W.J. McAdams	9
R.H. Pym	3	G. McElhinney	6
J. Seddon	6	R.J. Napier	1
A. Shepherd	1		
J. Smith	5	*Repulic of Ireland*	
J.W. Sutcliffe	4	O. Coyle	4
J.A. Turner	1	A.P. Dunne	8
D. Weir	2	C. Hurley	3
R. Westwood	6	J. McAteer	8
J.E. Wheeler	1	J. McDonagh	9

Scotland	
W.L. Cook	3
A. Donaldson	6
J. McGinlay	2
W. Moir	1
W. White	2

Wanderers' first player to be capped was Kenny Davenport who played against Ireland in 1890. He scored two goals in England's 9–1 win.

David Jack

David Jack is perhaps most famous for scoring the first goal in a Wembley Cup Final, but he contributed far more to the game than that.

Willie Cook—winner of three Scottish caps, he helped the Wanderers defeat Portsmouth in the 1929 Cup Final.

He was born in Bolton in April 1899, the son of former Wanderer Bob Jack. His football career took him from Leigh Road School, Southend to Plymouth Presbyterians, the Royal Navy and Plymouth Argyle, where his father was manager.

He played in Argyle's initial season in the Football League in 1920, his last goal for the club coming in a 3–1 home win against Gillingham in September that year.

Arsenal and Chelsea, with whom he had played during World War One, wanted him, but he chose the Wanderers and in December 1920, they paid a then record fee of £3,500 for his signature. He made his debut as inside-foward in a goalless draw at Oldham the following month and became a regular thereafter. For the next seven seasons he shared the goalscoring responsibilities with Joe Smith and was the club's top league scorer in five of them.

David Jack netted in six of Bolton's seven F.A. Cup ties on their way to winning the trophy for the first time in 1923. A year later, he won the first of four England caps whilst at Burnden. He scored the winner in the 1926 F.A. Cup Final, but in October 1928, he joined Arsenal for a then record £10,340 transfer and went on to win both League Championship and further F.A. Cup winners' medals with the Gunners.

He later managed Southend United, Middlesbrough and League of Ireland club, Shelbourne. He worked as a sportswriter before retiring in April 1955. Jack also worked for the Inland Revenue, as he had done in the early part of his career, before his death in September 1958.

Junior Whites

One of the biggest success stories of the 1978–79 season was the formation of the Junior Whites club. The club organised by Nat Lofthouse with Alan Gowling as its chairman, brought hundreds of youngsters under the wings of the Wanderers. Three enrolment nights were held and the club was packed to the seams on each occasion. The players did their best to make things go with a swing by attending the sessions and signing autographs.

The Junior Whites now in their 18th season, numbered around 606 members in the club's F.A. Cup run of 1993–94 and meet on the first Monday of each month in the club's Executive Suite.

Largest Crowd

It was on 18 February 1933 that Burnden Park housed its largest crowd. The occasion was the F.A. Cup fifth round match against Manchester City. The crowd was a staggering 69,912, Bolton losing the game 4–2 with Westwood and Milsom netting for the Wanderers.

Last Day Fate

On three of the six occasions that Bolton were relegated from Division One, their fate has been decided on the last day.

In 1908, the Wanderers needed only to draw their last game, but lost 1–0 to Notts County and went down. In 1933, Bolton knew a good last-day win *could* save them; they thrashed Leeds United 5–0, but as the other relegation candidates won, the Wanderers still suffered relegation. In 1964, the club should have fought clear, but inexplicably lost at home to Wolverhampton Wanderers 4–0 in the last game. So down we went again!

Yet none of these moments were as tragic as the manner in which the club slipped into the Fourth Division in 1987.

Late Finishes to a Season

Bolton's final play-off against Tranmere Rovers at Wembley Stadium on 1 June 1991 is the latest date for the finish of any Wanderers season. Previously 28 May 1989 had seen us beat Torquay United in the Sherpa Van Trophy Final.

If play-offs are excluded, Bolton's latest finish to a league season was 17 May in seasons 1962–63 and 1976–77 when we travelled to Ipswich Town (1–4) and Bristol Rovers (2–2) respectively.

During the War, many curious things occured, among them the continuance of the 1940–41 and 1944–45 seasons right into June. Thus Bolton's last competitive match in the 1940–41 season was on 7 June at Oldham Athletic (2–3) whilst on 2 June 1945, we won 2–1 at Chelsea.

Leading Goalscorers

The Wanderers have provided the country's leading goalscorer on three occasions. In 1905–06, Albert Shepherd scored 26 goals to share the honour with Bullet Jones of Birmingham City, whilst Jack Milsom scored 31 goals in 1934–35 as Bolton gained promotion from the Second Division. Frank Worthington was the last Bolton player to gain this distinction in 1978–79, when he scored 24 goals in the First Division.

Leyland DAF Cup

The Leyland Daf Cup replaced the Sherpa Van Trophy for the 1989–90 season.

The Wanderers began their defence of the newly named trophy with a 2–0 home win over Crewe Alexandra. Julian Darby and Nicky Brookman scored the goals, whilst Dave Felgate saved a penalty. Despite losing 1–0 at Wigan Athletic, the Wanderers still qualified for the knock out stages.

Two goals from David Reeves saw off a stubborn Lincoln City side at Burnden, whilst a Stuart Storer goal saw Bolton defeat Rotherham United 1–0 in the Northern Area quarter-final. Any hopes of a return to Wembley came to an end with a 2–1 defeat at Tranmere Rovers in the semi-final.

In 1990–91, one goal was enough to beat Tranmere Rovers at Burnden, but in the second preliminary round match, the Wanderers were crushed 3–0 at Blackpool.

Nat Lofthouse

Nat Lofthouse recalled that his first game of football was as an emergency goalkeeper and when he returned home, it was to be given a severe lecture from his parents for kicking out a brand-new pair of shoes!

Attending the same school as the legendary Tommy Lawton, he signed for the Wanderers in 1939.

His first game for the club was in March 1941, when at the age of 15 years 207 days, he scored twice as Bolton beat Bury 5–1 at Burnden Park in a Football League North game. The son of a Bolton coalman, he worked on the coalface during the war years, often going straight from the pit to assist the Wanderers in wartime games. He was on the field in March 1946, when 33 people lost their lives in the Burnden disaster. Nat was recognised at international level in November 1950 when he was chosen to lead England's forward line at Highbury in the

match against Yugoslavia. He fulfilled his promise by scoring both England's goals in a 2–2 draw in a game that was to be the first of a glittering career for England.

In May 1952, he earned the tag of 'Lion of Vienna' after his heroic performances against Austria when he scored twice in England's 3–2 win. The winning goal came nine minutes from time, as he collected a pass from Tom Finney and began a surging run that took him from the halfway line to the Austrian penalty area. As the Austrian goalkeeper charged out at him, Nat didn't falter and hit the ball cleanly into the corner of the net—the impact was such that when he and the goalkeeper collided, Nat had to leave the field for treatment.

In September 1952, he scored six goals for the Football League against the Irish League at Molineux.

He scored in every round of the 1952–53 F.A. Cup competition, but injury-hit Bolton lost 4–3 to Blackpool in the final. He was voted Footballer of the Year at the end of that season by the Football Writers' Association. In 1955–56, he was the leading goalscorer in the First Division with 33 goals.

In 1958, he captained Bolton to their F.A. Cup victory over Manchester United, scoring both goals in Wanderers' 2–0 win. His second became a major talking point, when he charged both the ball and United's Irish 'keeper Harry Gregg over the goalline. The shoulder charge was still much part of the game at the time and Nat's attitude that day was as it always was—he wanted to win by any fair means. And the referee ruled that what he did was within the laws.

On October 22 1958, Nat played his last game for England. His powerful running caused some anxious moments in the Russian defence. England were coasting 4–0, when in the last minute, Bobby Charlton found the big man with a good pass. The Bolton centre-forward fired in a splendid shot for the fifth goal, much to the delight of the crowd—it brought the loudest cheer of the afternoon.

He won 33 caps and scored what was then a record 30 goals for his country. A severely damaged ankle, incurred on Bolton's South African tour of 1959, threatened his career. But Nat the lion-heart refused to give up. He struggled to regain fitness and made several come-back attempts, but in 1961 he finally accepted defeat.

Bolton immediately appointed him assistant-manager and in 1968 he took over as manager. He had two separate spells as team-manager, in fact, before deciding to take a back seat. He returned to become

 Nat Lofthouse—Bolton Wanderers' most illustrious personality.

executive club manager and later president to continue his devotion to Lancashire's oldest club.

Thoughout his career, Nat Lofthouse gave total loyalty to Bolton Wanderers. His direct, yet stylish mode of play made him one of the world's great forwards of his age.

Bolton's full league record under Nat Lofthouse is:

P	W	D	L	F	A
107	30	31	46	134	167

Long Service

Nat Lofthouse is undoubtedly Bolton Wanderers' most illustrious personality. Having been with the club since 1939, first as a player and then as coach after his retirement through injury in 1960, he became team manager in 1968. Nat's 33-year association ended in 1972, but six years later he returned to become manager of the Executive Club. In December 1985 he took charge again, albeit for one game and in 1986 he capped what was almost a lifetime's service (49 years at the time of writing) by becoming the club's president.

Charles Foweraker was persuaded to become secretary, pro tem, when Tom Mather was called up in 1915. After guiding the club through the war years, he was appointed secretary-manager in 1919. He was in charge during the 1920s when the Wanderers won three F.A. Cup Finals at Wembley. He was awarded the Football League's long-service medal in recognition of more than 21 years in the Wanderers' employment. In August 1944, Foweraker retired through ill-health, having completed 49 years' continuous service with the club—he had entered football in a part-time capacity in 1895, acting as a checker when Burnden Park opened.

Walter Rowley went to Bolton from Oldham Athletic in 1912 and served the club well until he was forced to retire through injury in May 1925. He was appointed coach to the Reserves and first-team coach at the outbreak of the war. In 1944, he was promoted to secretary-manager, but six years later, resigned due to ill health and was awarded life membership of the club for services rendered in his 38 years.

George Taylor served the Trotters for over 50 years as a player, coach and scout. Playing the last of his 220 league games in 1945, he was appointed coach. Later he became chief coach, a position he held when Bolton won the 1958 F.A. Cup Final. In May 1967, he was awarded a testimonial and even after retirement still worked for the backroom staff on a part-time basis.

Bill Ridding's association with Bolton Wanderers began in 1946 when he was appointed trainer. In February 1951, Ridding was officially appointed secretary-manager—a position he didn't relinquish until August 1968. At the time of his departure, he was second only to

Matt Busby as the League's longest-serving manager. There are a number of Bolton players who have given long service to the club.

Ted Vizard who made 512 first-team appearances, making his last appearance in 1931 before taking charge of the 'A' team, gave almost 23 years' service to the club.

Other players include: Joe Smith (1908–1927) Jimmy Seddon (1914–1932) David Stokes (1902–1920) Roy Greaves (1965–1980) Alex Finney (1922–1937) Warwick Rimmer (1960–1974) and Bryan Edwards (1950–1965)

Loughborough Town

Loughborough Town spent five seasons all in the Second Division between 1895 and 1900, when they were not re-elected after finishing bottom of the table and winning just one game. It was in their last season (Wanderers first in the Second Division) that the two clubs met.

Laurie Bell signed from Everton in the close season, scored Bolton's first goal in a 3–2 win at Loughborough on the opening day of the season and then hit a hat-trick as the Wanderers overwhelmed their opponents 7–0 at Burnden Park.

Lowest

The lowest number of goals scored by Bolton Wanderers in a single Football League season is 28 in 1897–98. However, that was a thirty match season and in 1970–71, when the club were relegated to Division Three, only 35 goals were scored.

The lowest points record in the Football League occured in 1902–03 when the Wanderers gained just 19 points to finish bottom of the First Division from a thirty-four match programme.

Managers

This is the complete list of Bolton managers with the inclusive dates in which they held office.

Biographies of those who have made major contributions to the club are included in alphabetical order in this A–Z.

John Somerville	1908–10	Jimmy Meadows	1971
Will Settle	1910–15	Jimmy Armfield	1971–4
Tom Mather	1915–19	Ian Greaves	1974–80
Charles Foweraker	1919–44	Stan Anderson	1980–1
Walter Rowley	1944–50	George Mulhall	1981–2
Bill Ridding	1951–68	John McGovern	1982–5

 The present Bolton management team who hope to lead the club into the Premier League this season.

Nat Lofthouse	1968–70	Charlie Wright	1985
	and 1985	Phil Neal	1985–92
Jimmy McIlroy	1970	Bruce Rioch	1992—

Tom Mather

Born in Chorley, Tom Mather joined the Wanderers during Will Settle's reign and acted as secretary before being appointed secretary-manager in 1915.

His record as manager is a difficult one to quantify, due to the fact that all Bolton's games under his charge were played during the First World War. His term in office was one of the most difficult of any Wanderers manager, for there were many occasions when he did not know whether he would be able to field a full team!

Although Mather remained in name as manager until 1919, he had been called up by the Royal Navy and he was rarely seen at Burnden. His duties were carried out by his assistant Charles Foweraker, though in February 1919, the Bolton directors placed the management of the team in the hands of Ted Vizard. This however, was only an interim measure to see the club through their remaining wartime games.

After the war, Mather returned to football as secretary-manager of Southend United. He later became manager of Stoke City and in 1933 he led them to the Second Division title. Two years later, he left to manage Newcastle United, leaving the club in 1939. After the war, he managed Leicester City and Kilmarnock before settling in Stoke, where he died in March 1957.

The Matthews Final

May 2 1953 was a day which will live forever in the hearts of Bolton Wanderers' supporters—the F.A. Cup Final won 4–3 by Blackpool.

The Wanderers broke away to open the scoring after only 75 seconds. Holden on the right found Lofthouse in front of goal and he scored with a surprise shot from 28 yards which Farm in the Blackpool goal failed to gather as he seemed to have the ball covered. Blackpool drew level in the 37th minute when Hassall deflected a Mortensen shot that appeared to be going wide. The Wanderers though were soon ahead when Moir beat Farm after good work by Holden and Langton on the Bolton right. Eric Bell, the Bolton right-back had been injured and caused a re-shuffle of the Wanderers team, yet it was he who headed his team into a 3–1 lead.

With 66 minutes of the game gone, Matthews crossed and Stan Hanson in the Bolton goal failed to hold the ball as it dropped and Mortensen was too quick for the keeper, pushing the ball just inside the post. The equaliser came when Mortensen took a free-kick three yards outside the penalty area, hammering the ball home with Hanson unsighted.

There was no stopping the Blackpool outside-right with several players in the Bolton side limping.

With a minute to go, Matthews dribbled his way along to finish with a short pass to Bill Perry who smashed his shot into the net from five yards. The Wanderers had collapsed in one of the most exciting F.A. Cup Finals in history and Stanley Matthews had his Cup-winners' medal.

John McGovern

Despite having 14 months left of his contract with Nottingham Forest, John McGovern was allowed to leave the City Ground to become player-manager of Bolton Wanderers.

He had made 545 League appearances for Hartlepool, Derby County, Leeds United and Nottingham Forest and this experience was expected to help the Wanderers with their problems in midfield. However, the reputation and tradition of the Bolton club proved to be a handicap to McGovern throughout his reign as the Wanderers manager. At the end of his first season in charge, the Trotters lost their Second Division status. He had taken over a squad which had only just missed out on being relegated the previous season and there was no money available to recruit better players.

He took a voluntary drop in wages to help the Wanderers through its financial problems and ran in a fund-raising marathon, also organised individual kit sponsorship schemes and supporters' evenings.

During the 1983–84 season an influx of younger players brought some good results and positive play, but McGovern was to suffer the consequences of a poor run the following campaign which left the team six places from the foot of Division Three.

In January 1985, he parted company with the Trotters, after making only 16 League appearances in his two-and-a-half years as player-manager—a great disappointment for the supporters of the club.

Bolton's full league record under John McGovern is:

P	W	D	L	F	A
111	36	24	51	133	156

Jimmy McIlroy

Jimmy McIlroy was appointed chief coach to manager Nat Lofthouse in August 1970. A natural player, rarely caught in possession and with plenty of time on the ball, he had won 55 international caps for Northern Ireland, whilst starring as an inside-forward for Burnley and Stoke City.

When his playing days were over, McIlroy became manager of Oldham Athletic before returning to the Victoria Ground as Stoke's chief coach. He resigned his position there in 1969 and was out of the game until 4 November 1970, when he was officially appointed team manager at Bolton. He had assistance from coaches Jim Conway and Eddie Hopkinson. His first game in charge was a 1–0 defeat by Norwich City, which was followed by a 2–0 reverse at Millwall.

Incredibly on 22 November and after only 18 days in charge, the Irishman parted company with the club. No official reason was given, but offers had been invited for a number of key players. If they had left, it would no doubt have further weakened the team and it was obvious that McIlroy could not work within those constraints.

Bolton's full league record under Jimmy McIlroy is:

P	W	D	L	F	A
2	0	0	2	0	3

Jimmy Meadows

Jimmy Meadows' playing career began as a full-back with Bolton YMCA before he made his Football League debut with Southport. In March 1951, he moved to Maine Road and it was whilst he was with Manchester City that he won his only England cap in a 7–2 win over Scotland at Wembley in April 1955.

His first managerial post saw him take Stockport County out of the Fourth Division in 1967. Returning to Bolton as team manager in January 1971, he had been chief coach at Blackpool. Although Bolton won their first game under his charge, with a side that had been selected by Nat Lofthouse, Jimmy Meadows was never to taste success at Burnden Park.

In his short spell as manager, the club sold Terry Wharton and Paul Fletcher and attempted to sell John Byrom and John Manning, whilst he received transfer requests from Roy Greaves, John Hulme and John Ritson.

He even recruited Joe Lancaster, a former Olympic athlete, in an attempt to boost the Wanderers' training programme, but unfortunately, morale was at a very low ebb and on 6 April 1971, he resigned as the team slumped to the bottom of the Second Division.

Bolton's full league record under Jimmy Meadows is:

P	W	D	L	F	A
12	1	3	8	6	23

Most Goals in a Season

Bolton Wanderers scored 96 goals in 42 Division Two matches during 1934–35. They scored in every home match and failed in only three away games. Sixty three goals came at home and in eight games, 4 or more goals were scored. At Burnden Park, Barnsley were beaten 8–0 and Burnley 7–0. The Wanderers also won at Oldham on the opening day of the season by 4–1. Top scorer was Jack Milsom with 31 goals, while Ray Westwood had 30. Bolton finishing the season in second place to gain promotion to the First Division.

George Mulhall

As a player, George Mulhall was an exciting outside-left with Aberdeen and Sunderland and winning three Scottish caps. In October 1971, he joined Halifax Town as trainer-coach, before being appointed manager some eight months later.

Mulhall arrived at Burnden Park in 1974 as assistant to Ian Greaves, before leaving to become manager at Bradford City in 1978. He began his second spell on the Wanderers' management team in March 1981 and was appointed manager in June of that year.

At Burnden, he took over a club that was in turmoil. Cost-cutting exercises abounded—six players had been released on free-transfers, six more were available for transfer, whilst both the chief coach and scout had left!

The season was a catalogue of disasters, though the Wanderers managed to stay in Division Two by the skin of their teeth, thanks to two home wins in the final week of the season and Cardiff's failure to beat Luton Town at Ninian Park.

However, there was conflict between Mulhall and the directors when he was forced to add Paul Jones to the nine players he had decided should leave the club. In June 1982, he left the club, later scouting for Ipswich Town and becoming assistant-manager at Tranmere.

Bolton's full league record under George Mulhall is:

P	W	D	L	F	A
42	13	7	22	39	61

Phil Neal

Phil Neal began his League career with Northampton Town after signing professional forms in December 1968. After making 206 first-team appearances for the Cobblers, he was signed by Bob Paisley for Liverpool for £65,000 in October 1974.

He made his debut for the Reds against Everton the following month as a replacement for the injured Alec Lindsay at left back. He was an ever-present from his second appearance for the club in December 1974 until missing a defeat against Sunderland in October 1983, a run of 366 consecutive Legue matches.

An intelligent, positional player, he denied the winger any space. Though he was excellent in defence, his distribution was immaculate. He won almost every honour whilst playing for Liverpool, picking up seven Championship medals and was on the winning side in four League Cup Finals. He won a U.E.F.A. Cup winners' medal and four European Cup winner's medals—only an F.A. Cup winners' medal eluded him.

He is the most capped England right-back of all time with 50 caps to his name. He succeeded Graeme Souness as skipper for the 1984–85 season, but halfway through the following campaign, he left to join the Wanderers as player-manager.

At Bolton, he continued to play, lending his experience to the younger players. His first few years in management were quite eventful. He led the side to Wembley, where they lost 3–0 to Bristol City in the Freight Rover Trophy Final. The club were relegated to the Fourth Division for the first time in their history, but bounced back immediately at the end of the following campaign. There was another visit to the Twin Towers in 1989, Bolton beating Torquay United 4–1 to clinch the Sherpa Van Trophy. All in all, his career tally amounted to 915 League and Cup games and 94 goals, a remarkable tally for a defender who specialised in penalties.

At the end of the 1991–92 season he left the club. He had helped bring stability to the club, along with a measure of success, but the fact that the Wanderers were carrying one of their strongest squads of recent years, the expectations of the Bolton faithful, the pressure of poor results and declining attendances prompted the bombshell.

After a period of involvement with the England management team, he now manages Premier League side, Coventry City.

Bolton's full league record under Phil Neal is:

P	W	D	L	F	A
309	115	93	101	391	356

Neutral Grounds

Burnden Park has been used as a neutral ground for F.A. Cup matches on a number of occasions.

In 1899, the ground was awarded its first F.A. Cup semi-final, a replay between Liverpool and Sheffield United and the following November, Burnden was the venue for a Football League representative game against the Irish League.

In April 1901, the F.A. Cup Final replay between Tottenham Hotspur and Sheffield United took place. This historic occasion became known as 'Pie Saturday' on account of the catering miscalculations. A crowd of 50,000 had been expected, but only 20,470 turned up. One firm of pie-makers alone produced 13,000 while another prepared half-a-ton of sandwich meat. At night, two-penny pies were being remaindered at three for twopence and later given away!

During the 1960s, Burnden was honoured with selection for two F.A. Cup semi-finals. In 1966, Everton and Manchester United played off their tie, whilst four years later, a second replay between Manchester United and Leeds United took place.

In 1985, Rugby League came to town, when Swinton entertained Sheffield Eagles on the undersoil heated pitch when Station Road was snowbound. In recent years, Burnden has been the venue for the Finals and semi-finals of the Rugby League's major cup competitions. The *Wanderers* themselves have had to replay on a neutral ground a number of times:

Date	Opponents	Venue	FA Cup stage	Score
11 February 1897	Grimsby Town	Bramall Lane	Round 2	3–2
13 February 1915	Millwall	Ewood Park	Round 2	4–1
15 March 1926	Notts Forest	Old Trafford	Round 6	1–0
25 February 1935	Tottenham H.	Villa Park	Round 5	2–0
16 January 1939	Middlesbrough	Elland Road	Round 3	0–1
9 February 1953	Notts County	Hillsborough	Round 4	1–0
23 February 1959	Preston N.E.	Ewood Park	Round 5	1–0
12 February 1973	Cardiff City	The Hawthorns	Round 4	1–0
23 February 1976	Newcastle Utd	Elland Road	Round 5	1–2
			F. Lg. Cup stage	
18 October 1977	Fulham	St Andrews	Round 3	2–1

Our F.A. Cup semi-finals were of course played on neutral grounds. We played Sheffield Wednesday (1–2) at Perry Barr, Birmingham on 8 March 1890 and again at Fallowfield, Manchester on 10 March 1894, when we reversed the scoreline. The Owls were our opponents again for our third F.A. Cup semi-final at Goodison Park on 21 March 1896 when the game ended all square at 1–1. The replay was at the Town Ground, Nottingham where Wednesday won 3–1. In 1904, we beat Derby County 1–0 at the Molineux Ground, Wolverhampton. Our three semi-finals of the 1920s were as follows: In 1923, we beat Sheffield United 1–0 at Old Trafford, in 1926 we defeated Swansea Town 3–0 at White Hart Lane and in 1929 we beat Huddersfield Town 3–1 in a game played at Anfield.

In 1935 we drew 1–1 with West Bromwich Albion in a semi-final played at Elland Road, before going down 2–0 in the replay at the Victoria Ground, Stoke. In 1946 we lost by a similar score to Charlton Athletic in the semi-final held at Villa Park, before seven years later, defeating Everton 4–3 in a superb match played at Maine Road. This was also the venue in 1958 when we defeated Blackburn Rovers 2–1 with Ralph Gubbins grabbing both goals. Our F.A. Cup Finals at Goodison Park, Crystal Palace and Wembley also qualify for inclusion.

New Brighton Tower

The Wanderers met New Brighton Tower in their promotion season from Division Two in 1899–1900. Laurie Bell scored both goals in a 2–1 home win, but New Brighton won 3–1 on 16 April 1900—Bolton's only defeat in the last eleven games of that campaign. After finishing fourth in the Second Division the following season, they resigned from the League. A reformed club joined the Third Division (North) when it was extended to 22 teams in 1923–24; eventually losing their battle for League status in 1950–51.

Newport County

Newport County played more matches than any other ex-member of the Football League. In the 61 seasons after they joined the newly formed Third Division in 1920, they played 2,672 games.

The two clubs first met on 15 October 1983 when the Welsh side won 3–2 at Burnden, but the Wanderers won by the same score at Somerton Park later that season. The sides met for five consecutive seasons, Wanderers doing the 'double' in 1985–86 (Home 4–0 Away 1–0) and in 1987–88 (Home 6–0 with John Thomas grabbing a hat-trick and Away 1–0).

Newport lost their League place automatically after finishing bottom of the Fourth Division in that season of 1987–88.

Nicknames

Many players in the club's history have been known to supporters by their nickname.

One of the first was John Somerville whose defensive qualities at right-back were unquestionable, so much so, that he became known as 'Johnny Surefoot'.

Bob Brown known as 'Sparrow' throughout his career, took part in the opening League fixture at Burnden Park in September 1895. By the end of his career which also saw him play for Sheffield Wednesday, Third Lanark and Burnley, he had appeared in every position except goalkeeper and full-back.

Dick Pym, 'the Topsham Fisherman' was born in that Devon village and earned his living from the sea. He played in all three Wembley Cup Finals in the 1920s, keeping a clean sheet in each.

Roy Hartle who was rated as one of the finest full-backs to be denied an international cap was affectionately known as 'Chopper'.

In the Bolton line-up at the same time was Wyn 'the leap' Davies, his nickname being due to his amazing heading talents.

In recent years, John McGinlay who joined the Wanderers for £100,000 from Millwall is known as 'Super John'. He scored in both F.A. Cup ties against Liverpool in 1992–93 and the all important penalty goal that won promotion against Preston North End on the final day of the season, whilst former club captain, Phil Brown, now with Blackpool was affectionately known as 'the oldest swinger in town'.

Non-League

The Wanderers have faced non-league opposition on thirty-five occasions in the F.A. Cup, the last being in November 1993 when they narrowly defeated the only Scottish club in the competition, Gretna, 3–2.

Before the formation of the Football League, the Wanderers took part in the F.A. Cup competition for six seasons, but never progressed beyond the fourth round, that being in 1884 when Notts County ran out winners in a replay at Pikes Lane. The Wanderers final game in the competition as a non-league side came in December 1887, Preston ran out 9–1 winners at Deepdale, this being the club's heaviest defeat in the competition.

Linfield Athletic of Belfast were the first non-league club to put the Wanderers out of the F.A. Cup in November 1888. Bolton however did have some excuse for going down 4–0. They had to send their reserves to play the tie in Ireland as the first team were involved in a Football League game against West Brom on the same day.

In February 1890, the Wanderers recorded their best victory in any of the major competitions with a 13–0 F.A. Cup second round success over Sheffield United at Pikes Lane. The club reached the semi-finals that season only to go down 2–1 to Sheffield Wednesday, who were then members of the Football Alliance at Perry Barr in Birmingham.

Bolton have been knocked out of the F.A. Cup by non-league opposition on six occasions, the last being in January 1911 when Midland leaguers Chesterfield won 2–0 at Burnden. The Wanderers at the time were at the top of the Second Division but went down to two goals by part-timer Revill who was a coal miner.

In January 1914, Bolton entertained Swindon Town who were then leaders of the Southern League. The Wiltshire club had caused an upset by defeating Manchester United in the previous round. A crowd of 50,558 saw the non-leaguers take a 9th minute lead, but a Joe Smith hat-trick and another goal by Evan Jones saw Bolton win 4–2. The crowd that day ranks as the best against non-league opposition.

Since the War, the Wanderers have been drawn against non-league opposition on nine occasions and have managed to qualify for the next round at the first time of asking with one exception. In January 1964, the Wanderers needed a Francis Lee penalty to earn a replay against Bath City but ran out comfortable 3–0 winners in the replay at Burnden Park.

Penalties

The club's first-ever penalty kick awarded in a League match was against Everton in January 1892, unfortunately Bolton captain Di Jones missed it!

James Cassidy was the first player to convert a penalty for the club in the 2–0 win over Notts County at Pikes Lane on 26 March 1892.

Jack Feebury was noted for his powerful shooting and in August 1913 won a Players' Union kicking contest. His 80-yard right foot punt won him the title and, when challenged by a spectator to do the same with the other foot, he duly obliged. From 1919 he scored a number of penalties, but then went the way of penalty artists and missed one, handing the job to Frank Roberts.

Jimmy Seddon who went on to win three F.A. Cup winners' medals with the Wanderers had the misfortune to give away a penalty for handball on his debut against Middlesbrough in February 1914.

Joe Smith who was Wanderers' most consistent scorer until Nat Lofthouse, holds the record for the most penalties scored—33 in the League and 6 in the F.A. Cup.

Harold Hassall joined Bolton from Huddersfield Town and though he scored from the spot on seven occasions for the Wanderers, it was whilst he was at Leeds Road that he had the distinction of saving a penalty from the great Tom Finney—Hassall had to go in goal when the 'keeper was injured.

Francis Lee who scored from the spot 22 times in the League and 4 in Cup competitions was one of the game's most deadliest penalty takers, yet it is John Thomas who holds the record for the most penalties scored in a season—8 in 1987–88.

Pie Saturday

In 1901, Burnden Park was chosen as the venue for the Cup Final replay between Tottenham and Sheffield United. In eager anticipation of a bumper crowd—the first game was watched by 114,815 at Crystal

Palace—the town's tradesmen brought in massive stocks of pies and souvenirs. But the day turned into a disaster, for Bolton Railway Station was in the process of being rebuilt and the railway company refused to offer cheap-day excursion tickets. A lot of merchandise went to waste that day, known for years afterwards in Bolton as 'Pie Saturday'. There were undoubtedly more than the official gate of 20,740 present, perhaps up to 30,000, but still this represents the lowest crowd at an F.A. Cup Final in this century.

Pikes Lane

Among the many early grounds used by the Wanderers were the Park Recreation Ground and Dick Cockle's Field, until the club finally struck roots at Pikes Lane in March 1881.

Pikes Lane was notoriously very muddy ground and suffered from being at the foot of a hill, from where an excellent free view was to be had. In February 1884, 'Athletic News' reported that between 4,000 and 5,000 spectators had assembled on the slopes during Bolton's Cup replay against Notts County and an enterprising farmer charged them half the Pikes Lane entrance fee.

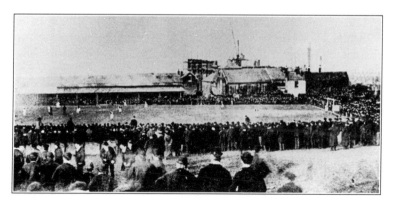

 Pikes Lane—a notoriously muddy ground.

Annual rent for the ground was £35 in 1881, but by 1893, with Bolton now in the Football League and enjoying higher gates, this rose to £175. The club began to look for a more suitable site and so Pikes Lane was last used in 1894–95.

The Wanderers wound up League Football at Pikes Lane in grand fashion. Cup finalists and eventual winners, Aston Villa were defeated 4–3, Notts Forest were thumped 4–1 on Good Friday the following day, the other cup finalists West Brom were drubbed 5–0. Peter Turnbull grabbed a second half hat-trick as Albion's 'keeper James Reader was sent off for pushing Willie Joyce.

This result ensured Bolton's safety from the test matches—seven wins and one draw in their last eight Pikes Lane appearances, pulled them through from an almost hopeless position!

Plastic

There have been four Football League clubs that replaced their normal grass playing pitches with artificial surfaces at one stage or another. Queen's Park Rangers were the first in 1981, but the Loftus Road plastic was discarded in 1988 in favour of a return to turf. Luton Town (1985), Oldham Athletic (1986) and Preston North End (1986) followed.

The Wanderers have never played on the Kenilworth Road or Boundary Park plastic. They visited the Loftus Road plastic on two occasions, losing 7–1 in 1981–82 and 1–0 the following season. The club has been a regular visit to Deepdale and though the Wanderers' record on their plastic pitch is not a good one, it is probably no worse than that of most clubs.

Wanderers' results on the Deepdale plastic:

1988–89	Lost	1–3
1989–90	Won	4–1
1990–91	Won	2–1
1991–92	Lost	1–2
1992–93	Drew	2–2

 John McGinlay, winner in 1994.

Player of the Year

Below is a list of winners of the Player of the Year Competition (Commercial) as other competitions such as the Supporters Club and Sponsors etc., have some seasons missing—ie: it wasn't held.

1978	Jim McDonagh	1987	Mark Gavin
1979	Frank Worthington	1988	David Felgate
1980	Neil Whatmore	1989	Mark Winstanley
1981	Alan Gowling	1990	Barry Cowdrill
1982	Paul Jones	1991	Tony Philliskirk
1983	Paul Jones	1992	Andy Walker

1984	Brian Borrows	1993	Andy Walker
1985	Simon Farnworth	1994	John McGinlay
1986	Asa Hartford		

Play-Offs

At the end of the 1986–87 season, the club finished in a relegation play-off position. Aldershot won the two-legged tie to send the Wanderers into the Fourth Division for the first time in their history.

Any hopes of automatic promotion in 1989–90 soon disappeared and there was only one victory in the final eight League games of the season, a 1–0 home success over Bristol City. A point from the final League game at Swansea put the Wanderers into the promotion play-offs.

A crowd of 15,105, the best of the season was at Burnden to see is Bolton could beat Notts County and keep their record of never having lost on a Sunday. A 1–1 draw left the Wanderers knowing they had to score in the second leg at Meadow Lane, but they had a hill to climb 90 seconds into the match when Tommy Johnson put County in front. Kevin Bartlett broke clear to score County's second in the 65th minute to secure County's passage to Wembley on a 3–1 aggregate.

At the end of the 1990–91 season, a single point stood between the Wanderers and automatic promotion to Division Two. Playing neighbours Bury, Tony Philliskirk's goal at Burnden Park before 19,198 was enough to see off the Shakers after a 1–1 draw at Gigg Lane.

A season of great expectation for the Wanderers ended in bitter disappointment when the ultimate prize of promotion was settled by a solitary incident.

Playing Tranmere at Wembley, Chris Malkin proved to be Rovers' matchwinner eight minutes into extra-time, the striker firing home a rebound after Felgate had blocked a Ged Brennan shot. Bolton then showed some of the determination that had seen them turn the previous October's relegation fears into February's promotion ambitions, but it wasn't to be. Julian Darby went close and there were fierce appeals when Mark Hughes appeared to handle after a collision. The

Whites continued to press, with Paul Comstive having the best chance to equalise, when he missed the target from 12 yards with only Eric Nixon to beat.

Points

Under the three points for a win system, which was introduced in 1981–82, the Wanderers best points tally was the 90 points in 1992–93 when the club gained promotion from the Third Division.

However, our best points haul under the old two points for a win system was 61 points also from 46 matches in our 1972–73 promotion season, which would have netted us 86 points under the present method.

Our worst record under either system was the meagre 24 points secured in 1970–71, though we only managed 19 points in 1902–3 (34 matches) and 1889–90 (22 matches).

Preston North End

The Wanderers and Preston North End have a tremendous history of games between the clubs that go back to before the Football League was formed in 1888. The first League meeting took place at Deepdale that year with North End winning 3–1, the second half of this game lasting only 40 minutes due to darkness! Two months later, North End visited Pikes Lane, attracting a crowd of 10,000 and the Wanderers despite holding a half-time 2–1 lead, eventually went down 5–2.

The Wanderers first League success over Preston came at the sixth attempt, when in November 1890, a Kenny Davenport goal separated the sides at Pikes Lane.

The Wanderers first League success at Deepdale didn't come until November 1896 when goals from Jocky Wright, Albert Gilligan and Billy Thompson earned a 3–2 win to put Bolton on top of the First Division. North End were also the first ever visitors to Burnden Park

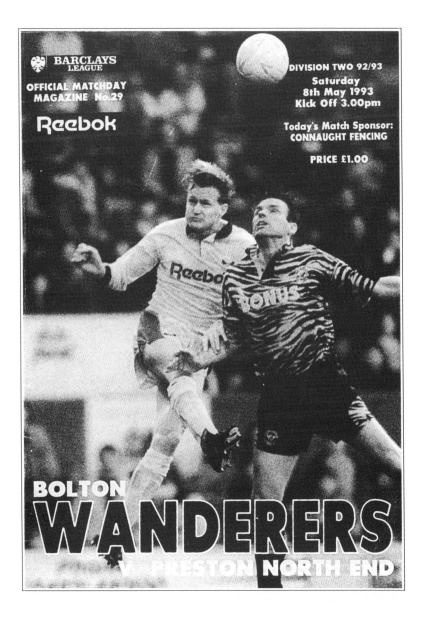

BOLTON WANDERERS

Football & Athletic Co. Ltd.

WINNERS OF THE
FOOTBALL ASSOCIATION CUP 1923, 1926 & 1929
F.A. Cup Finalists 1894, 1904, 1953.
FOOTBALL LEAGUE (NORTH) CUP 1944-45
LANC. CUP 1885-6, 1890-1, 1911-2, 1921-2, 1924-5, 1926-7, 1931-2,
1933-4, 1947-8
MANCHESTER CUP 1894-5, 1905-6, 1908-9, 1920-1, 1921-2
RICHARDSON CUP 1928-9, 1930-1. WEST LANCS. CUP 1930-1, 1950-1

Telephone: BOLTON 800   Telegrams: "WANDERERS, BOLTON"

DIRECTORS :
W. HAYWARD (Chairman), E. GERRARD, J.P. (Vice-Chairman),
C. N. BANKS, P. DUXBURY, Ald. J. ENTWISTLE, J.P.,
H. WARBURTON, A. E. HARDMAN.
W. RIDDING (Manager)   HAROLD ABBOTS (Secretary)

1953-54 SEASON
FUTURE EVENTS AT BURNDEN PARK:

Football League	Kick-off	Central League	Kick-off
Feb. 20—Portsmouth F.A. Cup	3-0	Feb. 27—Derby County Res....	3-0
Mar. 6—Sunderland...	3-0	Mar. 13—Blackpool Res. ...	3-0
Mar. 20—Aston Villa	3-0		

CANTEEN: TEA 3d. COFFEE 4d. HAM SANDWICH 6d

PROGRAMME of MUSIC	Selection ... COMMUNITYLAND No. 1 ... ...Rimmer
	Selection ... COMMUNITYLAND No. 2 ... ...Rimmer
played by	Waltz ... BLUE DANUBE... ... ... Strauss
	Selection .. OLD CHELSEA .. ..Coward
THE BOLTON BAND	March .. IMPERIAL ECHOES ... ... Alford

Sat. Feb. 13—PRESTON N. END

OFFICIAL PROGRAMME

in September 1895 when they won a friendly encounter thanks to a goal from David Smith.

The Wanderers best victory against Preston was in October 1924 when they ran up a 6–1 scoreline at Burnden with goals from David Jack (2) Joe Smith (2) Joe Cassidy and Ted Vizard. Bolton almost equalled this in September 1964 when two goals each from Wyn Davies and Freddie Hill and one from Francis Lee gave them a 5–1 success.

Despite the number of league games (116) between the clubs, there have been comparitevely few high scoring encounters, although in recent years there has nearly always been a result, as in May 1993 when a John McGinlay penalty sent the Wanderers into Division One and Preston into Division Three. But it wasn't the first time that a result at Burnden has sent the North End side down. In April 1961, a 1–1 draw resulted between the clubs, which was not enough to prevent North End dropping out of the First Division with relegation rivals Blackpool and Newcastle United picking up points on the same day.

Promotion

The Wanderers have won promotion nine times so far!

Having suffered relegation for the first time in 1899, Bolton set about ensuring their return to the top flight with the minimum of delay. The Trotters scored 79 goals—then a club record in League football and finished runners-up to Sheffield Wednesday.

P	W	D	L	F	A	Pts
34	22	8	4	79	25	52

Relegation came again in 1903 and this time it took Wanderers two seasons to win their way back again. Two more club records were smashed in 1904–5 as the Trotters scored 89 goals and collected 56 points.

P	W	D	L	F	A	Pts
34	27	2	5	89	22	56

After another relegation in 1908, the Wanderers won immediate promotion in spite of a very poor start to the season. Several new players were signed in mid-season and, by losing only one of the final twelve league games, the club clinched promotion by beating Derby County 1–0.

P	W	D	L	F	A	Pts
38	24	4	10	59	28	52

Sadly the Wanderers remained for only one season in the First Division, but again won an immediate return in 1910–11. The season reached a dramatic climax when Bolton travelled to Birmingham, needing a draw to guarantee promotion. We lost 2–1, but fortunately for us, so did our closest rivals Chelsea and as a result, we took runners-up place and promotion.

P	W	D	L	F	A	Pts
38	21	9	8	69	40	51

The Wanderers remained in the First Division until 1934 and it took two seasons to rebuild. Towards the end of 1933–34, the side found its confidence and finished unbeaten in its final 12 games. They carried this form into the following season to win promotion, beating West Ham to the runners-up spot. Jack Milsom was the Second Division's leading goalscorer with 31 goals, whilst Ray Westwood scored 30.

P	W	D	L	F	A	Pts
42	26	4	12	96	48	56

It wasn't until 1972–73 that the club experienced another successful promotion campaign. By then, the Wanderers had dropped into the Third Division. Under Jimmy Armfield's guidance, Bolton rose to the top of the table in November and subsequently never fell below third place. Four wins and a draw in the final five games ensured that the club went up as Third Division champions.

P	W	D	L	F	A	Pts
46	25	11	10	73	39	61

Further promotion was achieved in 1977–78 after three years of frustration. After missing by one point in 1975–76, the Wanderers suffered the same fate twelve months later. But justice was finally done in 1977–78 which opened with three wins in a row.

P	W	D	L	F	A	Pts
42	24	10	8	63	33	58

It was another ten years before the Wanderers won promotion again, but during that time, the club had slipped into the Fourth Division for the first time in its history. Some £30,000 was invested in bring Robbie Savage to Burnden from Bradford City and it was his goal in the final game of the season that gave Bolton victory at Wrexham to win the third promotion spot.

P	W	D	L	F	A	Pts
46	22	12	12	66	42	78

The club last won promotion in 1992–93 after suffering the disappointment of missing out in 1991 on goal difference and then losing out in extra time to Tranmere in the Wembley play-off. The arrival of Bruce Rioch and Colin Todd saw the team get back onto the right track by not only earning success but by gaining admirers in the way that it was achieved.

The season saw more club records tumble, the final win of the season, 1–0 at home to Preston was the 27th equalling a Club record set way back in 1905. The 18 home wins equalled the record set in 1924–25 and 1972–73 when the club won the Third Division championship.

A new points total of 90 was set up and, even if calculated on the old two points for a win system, would have overtaken the 61 points total of 1972–73.

P	W	D	L	F	A	Pts
46	27	9	10	80	41	90

Dick Pym

Dick Pym the 'Topsham Fisherman' was born in that Devon village in February 1893 and earned his living from the sea. Before becoming a goalkeeper, he played as an amateur centre-forward for Topsham.

In 1911, Pym signed for the Southern League Exeter City, and went on to make 186 consecutive appearances before in a cup-tie against Watford, he broke his collarbone.

Five years later, he joined the Devonshire Regiment and became a Sergeant P.T.I. In 1918 he was transferred to the 8th East Surrey Regiment and was later wounded in action.

It was in July 1921 that the Wanderers secured his transfer, after weeks of negotiation. Although the precise fee was never revealed, it was believed to be around the £5,000 mark, which was a record for both clubs at that time and a record for any goalkeeper.

He made his debut for the Wanderers in the 2–2 home draw with Preston North End and quickly settled in the team that won the F.A. Cup for the first time in 1923.

Pym's qualities were soon recognised and he appeared for the Football League in Belfast. Yet despite his sea-faring background, he was seasick on the crossing from Liverpool.

In February 1925, he won the first of his three England caps against Wales at Swansea. The following year, he collected another F.A. Cup Winners' medal as Bolton beat Manchester City 1–0 and despite injury, made it a hat-trick of Wembley wins in 1929—he kept a clean sheet in each final.

Dick Pym played his last game for the Wanderers in the 7–2 defeat at Anfield before returning to the fishing industry in Topsham, where he

remained until his death in September 1988, the last survivor of the 1923 side.

Re-election

At the end of the 1889–90 season, Bolton finished fourth from bottom of Division One on goal-average, the difference of one-hundredths of a goal being in favour of Aston Villa, thus leaving the Wanderers having to apply for re-election.

At the League meeting, the Trotters stated that their home defeat by Notts County had been by three goals and not four, therefore placing the Wanderers above Villa.

The League settled the matter by stating that only Bolton and Burnley had complied with the Secretary's request for an official return of results. It was agreed that both Villa and Wanderers should remain in the League without going to re-election—this is the closest the club have ever come to losing their League status.

Relegation

The Wanderers have on ten occasions experienced the anguish of relegation, less often than many clubs of a similar age. The first came in 1899 but on that occasion we were back in Division One within twelve months. We finished bottom of the First Division in 1903 and then it took the club two years to reclaim their place.

Further relegations in 1908 and 1910 were followed by instantaneous promotion and, when we went down again in 1933, it needed only two seasons to effect a recovery.

Relegation in 1964 was a prelude to our longest ever period of exile from top flight football. In 1971 we were relegated to Division Three for the first time and it wasn't until 1978 that the club returned to Division One. Another relegation came in 1980 and in 1983 we dropped back one more into Division Three. After finishing 21st in

1987, we were involved in the play-offs only to lose over two-legs to the now defunct Aldershot and enter the Fourth Division for the first time in the club's history.

Bill Ridding

Bill Ridding became one of the longest serving managers in the game at Burnden Park. He was appointed secretary-manager in 1950 and he remained in charge until his resignation in August 1968.

Ridding's association with Bolton Wanderers began in 1946, when

Walter Rowley appointed him trainer and, on Rowley's resignation some four years later, he was put in temporary charge.

The highlight of Bill Ridding's managerial career came in 1953 when he led the team out at Wembley for that magnificent F.A. Cup Final against Blackpool. That will always be remembered as one of the greatest Cup Finals of all. In 1958, he took the Wanderers to Wembley again with a team he had put together for £110 and this time had the pleasure of being on the winning side against Manchester United.

As a player, Bill Ridding had been a centre-forward, playing for Tranmere Rovers and both Manchester clubs before a double cartilage injury forced his retirement at just 22 years of age. In August 1968, he relinquished the manager's position to concentrate on his physio-

Bill Ridding, one of the longest serving managers in the game. He was manager of the Wanderers from 1951 to 1968.

therapy business, later joining Lancashire County Cricket Club in that capacity.

Dying in September 1981 at the age of 70, he was at the time of his departure, second only to Sir Matt Busby as the League's longest serving manager.

Bolton's full league record under Bill Ridding is:

P	W	D	L	F	A
729	274	174	281	1108	1128

Bruce Rioch

Bruce Rioch celebrated his first season as Bolton's manager by leading the club to promotion to the First Division in May 1993.

He started his footballing career with Luton Town in 1963 and went on to make 149 League appearances, scoring 47 goals. A goalscoring inside-left, he became an integral part of Allan Brown's Fourth Division championship-winning team of 1968. He played for one season in the Third Division before joing Aston Villa for £100,000. Villa's manager at the time was Tommy Docherty and Rioch followed Docherty into the Scottish national side. In fact, in a career which took him to Derby, Everton, Birmingham, Sheffield United and Torquay, he won 24 caps and had the honour of captaining his country.

Bruce Rioch closed his playing career with Torquay United and gathered his first experience of management with the Devon club. His first success—and this is a considerable achievement—came following his appointment by Middlesbrough in February 1986. Guiding the club from a dire financial position, he lifted them from the Third Division to the First within two seasons. However, Boro were relegated after only one year and Bruce left Ayresome Park in March 1990 when they were back in the Second Division. In less than a month, he was in charge at Millwall, arriving at The Den when the Londoner's relegation from Division One was already confirmed. They reached the play-offs in the following season.

Next stop for the former Scotland captain was Burnden Park in May 1992, following the departure of Phil Neal. He achieved promotion in

his first season in charge as his side finished as runners-up in Division Two. Not only did the Wanderers earn success, but gained many admirers in the way that it was achieved. A believer in bloodying youth, he has always produced hard running sides and his experience of manangement at this level is sure to stand the Wanderers in good stead.

Bolton's full league record under Bruce Rioch is:

P	W	D	L	F	A
92	42	23	27	143	105

Walter Rowley

Walter Rowley spent all his working life in football, including 38 years with the Wanderers as a player, coach and manager.

Born in Little Hulton, he showed early promise with local sides, Farnworth Wednesday, Walkden Wednesday and Little Hulton Wednesday. His first professional club was Oldham Athletic, from where Bolton signed him in August 1912.

After the war, he became a first-team regular, but was 12th man for the 1923 F.A. Cup Final, having just finished a six-week suspension after being sent off in the fifth round tie at Huddersfield.

In May 1925, injury forced him to retire and he was appointed coach to the Wanderers' reserves. At the outbreak of the Second World War, he was first-team coach and at the end of his first season in charge, the Wanderers won the Football League War Cup. He was promoted to secretary-manager on Charles Foweraker's retirement in August 1944, but on the return to normal League football he had the unenviable task of ending the careers of Albert Geldard, Harry Hubbick, George Hunt and Ray Westwood, as these older stalwarts had seen their best years.

Money was spent on players in an attempt to improve the Wanderer's First Division position, but in October 1950, Rowley was forced to resign due to ill health. Awarded life membership of the club for services rendered, he later returned to management with Middlesbrough and Shrewsbury Town.

Bolton's full league record under Walter Rowley is:

P	W	D	L	F	A
180	58	39	83	229	259

Rugby League

It was in 1985 that Rugby League came to Burnden Park. The club's undersoil heating proved to be a boon as Swinton were allowed to play their League game against Sheffield Eagles, when their Station Road pitch was snowbound.

Further Rugby League games followed, with some of the largest attendances seen on the ground in recent times being for the semi-finals and Finals of two of the Rugby League's major Cup competitions.

Second Division

Bolton Wanderers have had eight separate spells in the Second Division. Relegated at the end of the 1898–99 season, the club bounced back immediately to finish second in their first season in the Second Division. However, three seasons later, the Wanderers were back again and after a season in which they finished seventh, they again came runners-up in 1904–05 to clinch promotion.

The Trotters had three more seasons in the top flight before they were relegated for a third time, but won the Second Division championship in their first season with 52 points. Unfortunately, their return to Division One was short-lived, for after just one campaign, the Wanderers were relegated again. Undefeated at home during the 1910–11 season, the Wanderers finished second and were promoted.

There then followed 18 seasons in the First Division before Bolton were relegated at the end of the 1932–33 campaign. They finished third in the Second Division the following season, but went one better in 1934–35, scoring 96 goals in gaining promotion.

Another lengthy spell of 22 seasons of top flight football followed before Bolton were relegated in 1963–64.

Upon returning to the Second Division, Bolton suffered the ignominy of Third Division football from 1971–73 before returning as champions. After two mediocre seasons, the Wanderers played some very attractive football before returning to Division One at the end of the 1977–78 season.

The White's only lasted two seasons in the First Division before rejoining the Second Division in 1980–81. Relegation in 1982–83 saw us plummet towards Division Three and Four before reorganisation for 1992–93 saw us back in the Second Division. Finishing as runners-up to Stoke City, the Wanderers were promoted to the First Division.

Bolton's all-time record in Division Two is:

P	W	D	L	F	A
938	406	222	310	1451	1144

Semi-Finals

The Wanderers have appeared in a total of ten semi-finals in attempts to get to Wembley with only one game between them and the twin towers.

On 24 March 1923, the Wanderers defeated Sheffield United 1–0 with David Jack getting the goal in front of 72,000 at Old Trafford. The gates were closed an hour before kick-off in what was a record attendance for any match outside London.

The Wanderers were clear favourites to beat Second Division Swansea Town at White Hart Lane on 27 March 1926 and they made no mistake, winning 3–0 with Joe Smith (2) and Joe Baggert getting the goals.

On 23 March 1929 Wanderers came from a goal behind to beat Huddersfield Town 3–1. The talking point of the game was Harold Blackmore's equalising goal which screamed home from more than 40 yards.

As a Second Division side, the Wanderers took on First Division West Bromwich Albion at Elland Road on 16 March 1934. A 1–1 draw

resulted and a replay at the Victoria Ground, Stoke on 20 March 1934 saw a 49,110 crowd break the attendance record, but only for Wanderers to go down 2–0.

On 23 March 1946 the Wanderers faced Charlton Athletic at Villa Park. The joy at reaching this stage of the competition was stifled somewhat after the disaster at Burnden in the previous round. Strangely both teams had lost in the competition as earlier rounds were played over two legs. A couple of Chris Duffy goals saw the Londoners reach Wembley where they were defeated by Derby County.

Before the Wanderers played Everton at Maine Road on 21 March 1953, they were shown a film of the 1923 F.A. Cup Final. It seemed to do the trick as Bolton raced into a 4–0 half-time lead. The second half was a different story, Everton coming back with three goals, but the Wanderers held out for a 4–3 victory.

Taking part in their 12th F.A. Cup semi-final against Blackburn Rovers at Maine Road on 22 March 1958, it was Ralph Gubbins standing in for the injured Nat Lofthouse who scored both goals in Bolton's 2–1 win.

On 18 January 1977 Wanderers travelled to Goodison Park to take on Everton in the League Cup semi-final first-leg. Duncan McKenzie gave Everton a half-time lead, but just two minutes from time, Wanderers were awarded a free-kick from which Neil Whatmore rifled home the equaliser.

Bolton's dreams of Wembley faded as a 23rd minute goal from Bob Latchford in the second-leg at Burnden on 6 February 1977 settled the issue. Duncan McKenzie missed a penalty for Everton with the crowd of 50,413 never to be seen at Burnden again due to the safety limit.

Will Settle

Will Settle's association with Bolton Wanderers came from his father, Mr Miles Settle JP, who joined the club's directorate in 1895–96, the year that Burnden Park was opened and Bolton Wanderers became a limited company.

After three years on the board, Will Settle succeeded his father and served in the same capacity until January 1910, when he was appointed manager in place of John Somerville.

Settle could do little to prevent the Wanderers falling into Division Two at the end of his first season in office, but in 1910–11, he guided the Trotters to promotion at the first attempt. Almost as important as the Wanderers success during Settle's first year in charge was the discovery of Joe Smith and Ted Vizard, a new left-wing pairing that became the cornerstone of the 'new' Bolton Wanderers.

He wasn't afraid to invest in new players who he thought would improve the club's chances of success. Bentley, Donaldson, Fay, Glendenning, Lillycrop and Seddon were all brought to Burnden under his management and when he sold Tom Barber to Aston Villa, the profits paid for the roofing to the Great Lever Stand.

After two seasons back in the First Division, Settle was given a five-year contract, but he failed to see out that term.

He led the club to sixth place in Division One in 1914 and to their F.A. Cup semi-final in 1915, but then wartime football replaced the League and Cup and Settle ended his 17-year association under something of a cloud, after he found certain responsibilities taken from him.

Bolton's full league record under Will Settle is:

P	W	D	L	F	A
206	89	44	73	336	308

Sherpa Van Trophy

The competition for Associate Members of the Football League was from 1987–88, sponsored by Sherpa Van.

The Wanderers first match in the Sherpa Van Trophy was a goalless draw at home to Preston North End on 13 October 1987. The club was dismissed from the competition in the first round when Bury won by the only goal of the game at Gigg Lane.

In 1988–89, the Wanderers at times played so well that it seemed their name was on the trophy all along. Between Steve Thompson setting the ball rolling with his last minute penalty in the

first qualifying match and clinching a Wembley place—again from the penalty spot—at Blackpool, Wanderers led a charmed life in the competition.

It was Mark Winstanley with his 40-yard spectacular shot who turned Wanderers season on its head as the Whites came back from being 1–0 down with 15 minutes to go, to win 3–2. Phil Brown did a similar salvage operation at Crewe in the Northern Area semi-final. Blackpool midfielder Russell Coughlin will always be remembered for the miss that turned the Northern Final in Wanderers favour. When he almost hit the 'Normid' sign on the Co-op wall from the penalty spot, you got the impression that Bolton were on their way. Julian Darby gave Wanderers a 1–0 first leg lead to set up another extra-time thriller for the final leg at Bloomfield Road. Andy Garner put Blackpool level on aggregate before Steve Thompson's trusty right foot served him well—just as it had done four months earlier.

The Sherpa Final brought the Trotters victory as they recovered from going a goal behind to Torquay United and went on to win 4–1.

Torquay took the lead in the 23rd minute when their top scorer Dean Edwards headed home from close range. But the warning signs were all too apparent for Cyril Knowle's Fourth Division team when Julian Darby was given too much time to turn and equalise five minutes later. There was an element of luck in Bolton's most crucial strike—their second in the 63rd minute. Jeff Chandler's low shot was deflected off youngster John Morrison to leave 37-year-old goalkeeper Allen well beaten.

Two excellent saves by Dave Felgate gave Torquay more incentive to attack but that left huge gaps at the back and they were caught out twice in the last 12 minutes. First Chandler raced forward and found the unmarked Dean Crombie who netted easily in the 79th minute and then three minutes later substitute Stuart Storer crossed for Trevor Morgan to hit the fourth.

The Bolton fans began to celebrate a victory which not only gave the Wanderers the Sherpa Van Trophy, but also established a new club record of 20 games without defeat. Four months earlier, such triumphs and records had been nothing but a pipe dream.

Joe Smith

Joe Smith was born in Dudley in June 1889 and was a Newcastle St Luke's player when he was awoken one August morning in 1908 by Bolton trainer George Eccles. He was offered 50 shillings (2.50) a week to sign and made his league debut in April 1909 at West Bromwich Albion.

Smith won his first England cap in February 1913 and continued his international career after the war, but due to the hostilities he was limited to five appearances overall.

Smith played in 51 wartime games for the Wanderers, scoring 48 goals, including six against Stoke City in September 1916 as Bolton won 9–2. He guested for Chelsea along with Ted Vizard, whilst serving in the R.A.F. and in 1918 they both helped the Pensioners win the London *v.* Lancashire Cup Final.

OGDEN'S CIGARETTES.

JOE SMITH.
BOLTON WANDERERS.

He was Bolton's most consistent scorer until Nat Lofthouse, and his 38 goals (which included hat-tricks against Middlesbrough, Sunderland and Newcastle) in 1920–21 are still a club record. In 1923 came Joe Smith's greatest honour when he was the first F.A. Cup Final captain to receive the trophy at Wembley. Three years later, he lifted the Cup again, but his career at Bolton was coming to an end.

After heading the Wanderer's League scoring charts for the sixth time, he joined Stockport County in March 1927 for £1,000. For the Edgeley Park outfit he scored 61 goals in 69 League games. In 1929, he joined Darwen and had a spell at Manchester Central before becoming manager of Reading in 1931. Four years later, he became Blackpool's manager, a position he held

until April 1958 when he was the longest-serving manager in the League. He guided the Seasiders to their best-ever league position and to the 1948, 1951 and 1953 F.A. Cup Finals.

He lived in Blackpool until his death in August 1971 at the age of 82.

John Somerville

John Somerville joined the Wanderers in March 1890 from his native Ayr and as a player, he saw both an F.A. Cup Final appearance and promotion to Division One. He became player-secretary in 1898 and had therefore been acting as secretary before he was appointed Bolton's first secretary-manager for the start of the 1908–09 season.

His first season as secretary-manager proved extremely successful as Wanderers collected their first championship trophy, winning the Second Division title after only a season's absence from the top flight.

Somerville had spent over £3,000 in transfer fees, bringing in James Hogan, Billy Hughes and Billy Hunter, a large sum in those days and had been rewarded for his calculated gamble.

The following campaign of 1909–10 however, proved to be a complete contrast, when Somerville found that the players who had helped the club to promotion were not good enough to keep the Wanderers in the First Division.

In January 1910 with Bolton at the foot of the First Division and beaten 4–1 by Second Division Stockport County in the F.A. Cup, the managership of the club was handed to Will Settle.

John Somerville remained as Wanderers secretary until the end of the season, terminating his contract in July 1910. Having served the club for twenty years, he went on to become a Football League linesman.

Bolton's full league record under John Somerville is:

P	W	D	L	F	A
60	28	6	26	85	73

Sponsors

The first name ever to be featured on the famous white shirts of Bolton Wanderers was Knight Security. The other sponsors have been Bolton Evening News, T.S.B., H.B. Electronics and Normid, whilst the club's current sponsors are Reebok.

Substitutes

Substitutes were first allowed in the Football League in season 1965–66. The first appearance of a substitute in League Football came at Burnden Park when Charlton Athletic's Keith Peacock came on during Wanderers' 4–2 win. Bolton's first substitute was Gordon Taylor who came on for John Napier in the club's 11th game of the season, a 3–2 home defeat by Southampton. We had to wait until the seventh game of the 1969–70 season for our first goalscoring 12—Gordon Taylor scoring the opening goal in the 2–0 win over Birmingham City.

The greatest number of substitutes used in a single season by the Wanderers under the single substitute rule was 27 in 1985–86, but since 1986–87, two substitutes have been allowed and in 1991–92, we used 63 in 46 matches.

The greatest number of substitute appearances for the Wanderers has been made by Stuart Storer who came on during 27 League games with 6 more appearances in cup-ties.

It was in 1991–92 that David Reeves caused us to re-write the Wanderers records on the matter of substitutes with an extraordinary 14 League appearances in the number 12 shirt.

Sunday Football

The first-ever Sunday matches in the Football League took place on 20 January 1974 during the three-day week imposed by the Government, during the trial of strength with the coalminers.

Bolton entertained Bristol City on that date and were successful by 2–1. In the club's other Sunday League match that season, the Wanderers travelled to Swindon Town and drew 2–2 with Neil Whatmore scoring both goals.

Bolton had in fact played on Sunday 6 January that year at home to Stoke City in the Third Round of the F.A. Cup and created history by arranging the first major professional soccer match on the Sabbath. The hero of the tie was John Byrom who hit a hat-trick in Bolton's 3–2 win.

Since then, the Wanderers have taken part in a number of Sunday games and have remained unbeaten, although there have been mixed fortunes.

In April 1981, a 2–2 draw with Orient at Brisbane Road secured Second Division safety after a relegation battle, but in May 1987, a 2–2 draw with Aldershot at Burnden after extra-time wasn't enough to save the Wanderers from relegation to the Fourth Division in a play-off encounter.

In May 1989, a visit to Wembley for the final of the Sherpa Van Trophy saw the Wanderers run out 4–1 against Torquay United.

In season 1991–92, an F.A. Cup victory was earned against Emley on a Sunday, whilst the best Burnden crowd of the season, 20,136 saw the Wanderers fight back to earn a 2–2 draw with Southampton in the Fifth Round of the F.A. Cup. In 1992–93, the Wanderers drew at home with Liverpool 2–2 before winning the replay, whilst goals from Green and McGinlay won the Fourth Round tie at Molineux.

Last season the Wanderers beat Notts Forest (4–3) and Tranmere Rovers (2–1) in front of Sunday's T.V. cameras and then an Alan Stubbs goal accounted for Aston Villa in the live Fifth Round F.A. Cup tie.

Suspensions

Jim McGeachan who came south from Scottish side Hibernian in November 1894 was suspended three years later by the Wanderers for refusing to travel to Sheffield. Bolton-born Sam Greenhalgh fell into dispute with the club in 1912 when he was suspended for refusing to play on the wing in an emergency. After serving his six weeks' ban, he sent his apologies to the board of directors and resumed his place in the side.

Frank Roberts would almost certainly have been a member of the Wanderers' successful Cup sides of the 1920s, but for his insistence on taking over the management of licensed premises in 1922, which was against club rules. He was suspended and joined Manchester City, being their leading scorer in 1925, 1926 and 1928, as well as playing against Bolton at Wembley in 1926.

Gareth Williams was suspended in November 1969 for refusing to train, whilst claiming that he was being made the scapegoat for Bolton's poor results. The Welsh-speaking Williams never fulfilled his promise at Burnden and joined Bury for £5,000. After only 42 appearances for the Shakers, he retired to join the prison service. Later he took over the management of a Fylde coast hotel before moving to run a bar in Gran Canaria!

Sustained Scoring

Wanderer's strikers Harold Blackmore, Nat Lofthouse and Francis Lee all scored 9 goals in 7 consecutive games. Blackmore's came in the 1930–31 season and included a hat-trick in a 6–2 win over Sheffield United. Lofthouse's came at the start of the 1956–57 season from the third game after he'd hit a hat-trick in the opening fixture. Francis Lee's came in the 1967–68 season and included a goal at Anfield in the League Cup.

However, it is David Weir who holds the club record in this section, as in 1889–90, he scored 15 goals in 7 consecutive games, including 4

Harold Blackmore, who scored 9 goals in 7 consecutive games, including a hat-trick in a 6–2 victory over Sheffield United.

against Belfast Distillery in a 10–2 win and 4 against Sheffield United in the club's record 13–0 victory.

At the start of the 1992–93 season, Andy Walker became the first player for nearly thirty years to have scored in the opening four league games. The last time it was achieved was in 1964 when Wyn Davies opened with a goal blitz and before that only two other Wanderers players have bettered that.

Joe Smith scored in the opening five games of the 1914–15 season and Jackie Milsom was on target in the first six games of the 1934–35 campaign.

John Sutcliffe

John Sutcliffe was one of three players to win England honours at both rugby and soccer. Born at Shipden near Halifax, he played for Bradford and Heckmondwike Rugby Union Clubs and won an England cap against New Zealand in 1889. In autumn

of that year, Heckmondwike were suspended for professionalism and Sutcliffe turned to soccer.

He joined the Wanderers but in an attempt to strengthen the forward line, his rugby instincts were obvious and he switched to goalkeeper. He made his full league debut for the club in December 1889 in a 7–0 win over West Bromwich Albion at Pikes Lane.

In March 1893, he made the first of five England soccer appearances and was always on the winning side for his country. He also made three appearances for the Football League side.

An all-round sportsman, Sutcliffe was the fastest player in the club over 120 and 440 yards and proved it in the club's sports day in 1890. Playing cricket for Great Lever C.C. he had the best batting average.

In January 1902, Sutcliffe became the first Bolton player to be sent off at Burnden Park. During a 3–1 win over Sheffield Wednesday, he was given his marching orders for bad language directed at the referee after the official allowed a goal that Sutcliffe claimed did not cross the goal-line. He was later suspended for 14 days.

After problems over wages and a benefit, he joined Millwall for £400 in May 1902, after making 364 League and Cup appearances for the Wanderers.

In May 1903, he signed for Manchester United after his request to rejoin Bolton was turned down.

A year later, he joined Plymouth Argyle, going on to make 166 appearances for the then Southern League outfit, before becoming coach to Southend United in 1911 and Arnhem, Holland in 1914. After the war, he was appointed trainer at Bradford City. He died in July 1947.

Television

Freddie Hill scored the only goal of the game against Blackpool on Friday 9 September 1960 in what was the first televised Football League game to be shown 'live'. There was then no more 'live' television of League games until the early 1980s.

Third Division

The Wanderers were relegated to the Third Division for the first time in their history at the end of the 1970–71 season.

The club's first game in the Third Division saw the Wanderers draw 2–2 at Oldham with John Byrom grabbing both Bolton goals. Jimmy Armfield had been appointed manager and he instilled some confidence back into what had become a lacklustre club. In his first season, he built a solid defence, the Trotters goal against column being bettered only by champions Aston Villa and third-placed Bournemouth. During 1972–73 the club won the Third Division championship—the youth policy which had been the foundation stone of the promotion also produced entertaining and sometimes spectacular football.

The Wanderers second spell in the Third Division came after the club's relegation in 1982–83. It was a bitter coincidence that relegation was suffered on the same ground and by the same result as 1971—4–1 at Charlton Athletic.

It was a young and inexperienced squad that opened the club's Third Division campaign in August 1983—the highlight of the season being the 8–1 thrashing of Walsall with Tony Caldwell, a £2,000 buy from Horwich R.M.I. scoring five.

In 1986–87, the club were relegated to the Fourth Division but won promotion at the first time of asking.

The Wanderers third spell in this Division lasted for five seasons until promotion was achieved in 1992–93. Phil Neal had laid the foundations for a steady season by season improvement. The club missed out on promotion in 1991 on goal difference and then losing out in extra-time to Tranmere in the Wembley play-offs.

The arrival of Bruce Rioch and Colin Todd got the team onto the right track not only by earning success, but by the way it has been achieved. Records tumbled in 1992–93—the final win of the season against Preston was the 27th, equalling a Club record set in 1905; the 18 home wins equalled the Club record set in 1924–25 and 1972–73 and a new points total was set up, the total of 90 being seven better than that of 1990–91 and even if calculated on the old two points for a win basis would have overtaken the 1973 sides total of 61 points.

Bolton's full playing record in the Third Division is as follows:

P	W	D	L	F	A
508	200	136	182	670	596

Transfers

The transfer of players has always been a feature of football and undoubtedly Wanderers' first major involvement in a transfer was when David Jack joined the club from Plymouth Argyle in December 1920 at a fee of £3,500. When he left in October 1928 to join Arsenal, the fee of £10,340 was a record.

In March 1962, the Wanderers accepted Everton's offer of £35,000 their largest incoming fee for the transfer of Dennis Stevens. Within two days of Stevens' departure for Goodison, Wyn Davies joined the Wanderers. A regular for four and a half years, his name became linked with almost every First Division club and in October 1966, Newcastle United paid £80,000 for him. A year later, Francis Lee joined Manchester City for £60,000—his sale prompting the Wanderers to enter what was then the biggest spending spree in their history as within the space of weeks, Gareth Williams was recruited from Cardiff City for £50,000 and Terry Wharton from Wolves for £70,000—a club record.

During the 1970s, Bolton signed internationals Tony Dunne and Willie Morgan on free-transfers and Peter Thompson from Liverpool for a bargain £18,000.

Frank Worthington (£90,000) and Alan Gowling (£120,000) had joined the Wanderers in 1977–78 and were the scourge of the First Division defences. Bolton's record transfer was increased again when they spent £250,000 on Neil McNab from Tottenham Hotspur. The following season, the club paid out what is still their highest fee for an incoming deal, £350,000 to bring Len Cantello from West Bromwich Albion. At the beginning of the 1981–82 season, Neil Whatmore joined Birmingham City for £340,000.

In recent years, Andy Walker was signed from Celtic for a bargain £160,000 whilst present manager Bruce Rioch's signings include: David Lee (£300,000 from Southampton), Owen Coyle (£250,000

from Airdrie), Jimmy Phillips (£300,000 from Middlesbrough) and John McGinlay (£140,000 from Millwall).

Undefeated

Bolton Wanderers have remained undefeated at home throughout two league seasons: 1910–11 and 1920–21.

The club's best and longest undefeated home sequence in the Football League is of 27 matches between 24 April 1920 and 15 October 1921.

The Wanderers' longest run of undefeated Football League matches home and away is 20 between 11 March 1989 and 16 September 1989.

Utility Players

A utility player is one of those particularly gifted footballers who can play in several, or even many different positions.

Probably the Wanderers earliest utility player was Tom Buchan who, between 1914 and 1923, played in every position apart from full-back. He even turned out as emergency goalkeeper in a 4–2 reverse at Stockport in November 1915 and in a 3–2 win on the same ground exactly two years later.

Don Howe spent his entire League career with Bolton. He made his debut in 1936, taking over the right-wing position from Jack Rimmer in a 0–0 draw at Anfield. Upon Rimmer's return, a place for Howe was always found and by the end of the 1936–37 season, he had played in every forward position except centre forward. He later proved himself capable of filling any position before settling at wing-half and becoming club captain.

John Wheeler and Derek Hennin two of the club's wing-halves in the 1950s showed their versatility when they turned out as emergency centre-forwards, each scoring a hat-trick! Wheeler hit three in Bolton's 4–0 win over Blackpool on 3 January 1953, whilst Hennin's treble came

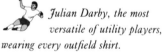 *Julian Darby, the most versatile of utility players, wearing every outfield shirt.*

in the match against Aston Villa on Good Friday 1958 as the Wanderers won by the same scoreline.

After about the mid 1960s, players were encouraged to become more adaptable and to see their roles as less stereotyped. At the same time however, much less attention came to be paid to the implication of wearing a certain numbered shirt and accordingly, some of the more versatile players came to wear almost all the different numbered shirts at some stage or another, although this did not necessarily indicate a vast variety of positions.

Peter Nicholson was certainly talented enough to wear all the Wanderer's outfield shirts during his career with the Trotters and Roy Greaves wore eight of them as he translated from striker to midfield.

However, in the modern game, probably Julian Darby now of Coventry City, has been the most versatile Bolton player, wearing every outfield shirt.

Victories

In a Season

The Wanderers greatest number of victories in a season is 27 in seasons
1904–5 and 1992–93, whilst the most home victories (18) has been
achieved on three occasions. The best of these was from 21 matches in
1924–25, but was also reached from 23 matches in 1972–73 and
1992–93.

In a Match

Wanderers best victories in the major competitions are as follows:

Home

Football League	8–0 *v.* Barnsley in Division 2	6 October 1934
F.A. Cup	13–0 *v.* Sheffield United in Rd 2	1 February 1890
F. Lg. Cup	6–2 *v.* Grimsby Town in Rd 2	26 October 1960

Away

Football League	7–1 *v.* Aston Villa in Division One	26 December 1914
F.A. Cup	5–1 *v.* Charlton Athletic in Rd 3	3 January 1933
F. Lg. Cup	4–0 *v.* Rochdale in Rd 2	10 October 1973

Ted Vizard

Born in Cogan, Cardiff, Ted Vizard played rugby for Penarth and football for Barry Town. He was recommended to the Wanderers by an old schoolfriend and invited for a month's trial. Bolton signed him in September 1910 and he made his debut in November that year in a 3–0 win against Gainsborough Trinity at Burnden.

The first of his 22 Welsh caps came in 1911, only two months after his League debut and his last in October 1926, when he was 37.

During World War, Ted Vizard served in the R.A.F. and guested for Chelsea alongside Wanderer's Joe Smith. The pair formed an ideal partnership and helped the London side win the 1918 London *v.* Lancashire Cup Final.

In February 1919, the management of Bolton Wanderers was put in Vizard's hands until normal League football returned and Charles Foweraker was appointed.

PLAYER'S CIGARETTES.

E. T. VIZARD.

Ted Vizard was a member of Bolton's successful F.A. Cup-winning teams of 1923 and 1926.

Though not a prolific goalscorer, his best season was in 1925–26 when he scored 13 goals, including all three in the 3–0 defeat of Arsenal.

He made his last appearance for the Wanderers on 21 March 1931. He was then 41, which makes him the oldest player to appear in a first-team game for the Trotters. He took charge of the 'A' team before leaving Bolton in April 1933 after almost 23 years' service.

Vizard became manager of Swindon Town and later took charge of Queen's Park Rangers and Wolves before becoming 'mine host' at a Tattenhall Hotel in 1950. He died in Wolverhampton in December 1973, aged 84.

Wartime Football

First World War

In spite of the outbreak of war in 1914, the major football leagues embarked upon their planned programme of matches for the ensuing season and these were completed on schedule at the end of April the following year. On Boxing Day that season, the Wanderers recorded their best away league victory with a 7–1 beating of Aston Villa. The F.A. Cup semi-finals were also reached, but we were beaten 2–1 by the eventual winners, Sheffield United.

The following season saw the introduction of regional leagues with games being allowed only on Saturdays and public holidays. In the first of these competitions, the Wanderers did badly and were second from bottom in the Lancashire section. By the last year however, they had worked themselves up the table and were then fourth.

Second World War

In contrast to the events of 1914, once war was declared on 3 September 1939, the Football League programme of 1939–40 was immediately suspended, and the Government forbade any major sporting events so that for a while there was no football of any description.

The Bolton team spent much of the war together in the 53rd Regiment R.A. (Bolton Artillery) and were involved in the Dunkirk evacuation and Middle East and Italian campaigns. In December 1939 the Wanderers entertained the 53rd R.A. who were on leave in what was virtually a current Wanderers XI *v.* Old Wanderers XI—the score 3–3 in front of 1,509 spectators.

Though Burnden Park was a deserted place during the war, the playing area was used by the Education Authority and the stands used by the Ministry of Supply to store food.

The Wanderers resumed playing on Christmas Day 1940 with a friendly at Blackpool. On 22 March 1941, Bolton beat Bury 5–1 with Nat Lofthouse at the age of 15 years 207 days grabbing the last two goals on his debut. In 1942, the Wanderers recruited Tom Finney from

Preston North End as a guest for a game at Burnley which Bolton won 2–1 with both goals scored by Nat Lofthouse. On 18 December 1943, Bolton lost their popular captain, Harry Goslin, who was killed in the Italian campaign. In August 1944, Charles Foweraker handed over the reins to Walter Rowley and six months later, the club won the Football League North Cup.

On 2 June 1945, Bolton visited Stamford Bridge for the North *v.* South Cup Winners' Final. The proceeds went towards the King George VI Fund for sailors, as Bolton coming from behind, beat Chelsea 2–1. The players received saving certificates instead of medals for victory.

White Horse Final

Bolton Wanderers 2, West Ham United 0

This was Wembley's first full final and it nearly became a disaster. Though 126,047 people paid for admission, thousands more burst

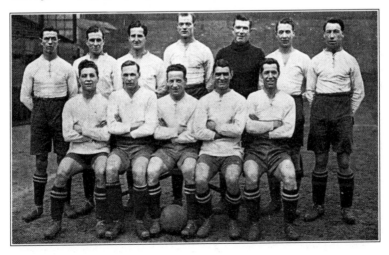

The victorious Bolton side that played in that historic first Wembley final in 1923.

down the doors to invade the stadium. It is believed that almost 200,000 were present at kick-off time when the pitch was completely covered by spectators!

As the Bolton players stood on the edge of the pitch watching the police horse clear the playing area, someone tapped Jack (JR) Smith on the back. It was his brother, whom he hadn't seen for six years!

It was largely due to the patience of the famous policeman on his white horse that the pitch was cleared, but even so, spectators still encroached onto the pitch during play. However, it was felt safer to play the game than to announce to the horde that the match would be postponed.

PLAYER'S CIGARETTES

HAWORTH · FINNEY · PYM · NUTTALL · JENNINGS · SEDDON · BUTLER · VIZARD · JACK · SMITH (J. R.) · SMITH (J.)

ASSOCIATION CUP WINNERS
BOLTON WANDERERS. 1923

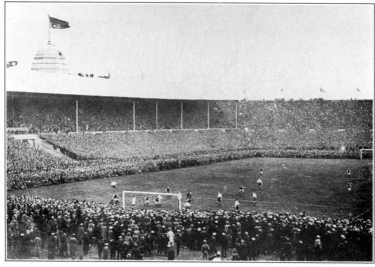

Action from Wembley's first final in 1923, Bolton beating West Ham United 2–0.

Within two minutes of the eventual kick-off which was delayed by 40 minutes, David Jack had scored for the Wanderers. Both teams remained on the pitch at half-time and eight minutes after the break, Bolton scored again. Taking a pass from Ted Vizard, J.R. Smith rammed the ball home with his left foot with such force that it hit the crowd wedged behind the goal and rebounded onto the pitch. Many people didn't know a goal had been scored until West Ham kicked off again.

Thus, in such bizarre circumstances, did Bolton secure the F.A. Cup for the first time in their history.

Wolverhampton Wanderers

There have been more than 40 instances of clubs meeting each other in four different divisions of the Football League, but there has been only one instance of two teams meeting each other in Divisions 1, 2, 3 and 4. When Bolton and Wolves met in the First Division 1979–80 (0–0 and 1–3) it was their last meeting until 1982–83 when they were both in the Second Division (0–1 and 0–0). When they next met in 1985–86, it was in the Third Division (4–1 and 2–0) and their next meeting in 1987–88 was in the Fourth Division (1–0 and 0–4). What price their next meeting being in the Premier League?

Worst Start

The club's worst ever start to a season was in 1902–03. It took 23 League games to record the first victory of the season, drawing just 3 and losing 19 of the opening fixtures. The run ended with a 3–1 success at Notts County on 17 January 1903 and the next four games were all won!

Despite an improved run-in towards the end of the season, relegation to Division Two wasn't avoided.

Frank Worthington

Frank Worthington became a hero at Burnden Park in what was a relatively short career there. From a footballing family—older brothers Bob and Dave, both full-backs, had long League careers—Frank started his career with Huddersfield Town in 1963 and turned professional in November 1966. He made 171 League appearances for Huddersfield, helping them win the Second Division title in 1970.

At the end of the 1971–72 season, Huddersfield finished bottom of the First Division and the chance came for him to join Liverpool. A fee of £150,000 had been agreed and Worthington duly arrived at Anfield to sign. He was a Liverpool player, subject to a medical examination. The club doctor revealed that Frank had high blood pressure—he had

 Frank Worthington—seen here with Neil Whatmore after scoring against Mansfield Town.

failed the medical. Leicester City seized their chance and a cut-price Worthington moved on for £80,000. In 1974, Frank's elegantly effective centre-forward play was rewarded with an England call-up from Sir Alf Ramsey. He held his place under caretaker manager Joe Mercer and went on to make eight appearances. Frank was at that time an international class player and should have made many more appearances for his country.

His old Huddersfield Town boss Ian Greaves was searching for that extra quality to lift the Wanderers into the First Division after two agonising near-misses. He came to Bolton on loan in September 1977 and scored on his debut against Stoke City. He was signed permanently for £90,000 and soon rediscovered the style which had made him one of the best strikers in the game—ice-cool finishing, the keen positional sense, the close control in tight spots and the neat headed flick-ons. Frank and his co-striker Neil Whatmore banged in 30 goals between them as Wanderers took the Second Division title. It was his goal at Blackburn that finally clinched the promotion.

The following season, Frank proved his class both as a target man and a finisher. Although Bolton struggled against relegation for a while, Frank ended the season with 24 league goals to top the First Division goalscoring charts. Bolton did the double over Manchester United that season, winning 3–0 at Burnden and 2–1 at Old Trafford, with Frank hitting two goals in each match; the second in injury time at Old Trafford took him past his career-best total for a season. His televised goal against Ipswich Town that season won the Goal of the Season competition.

In October 1980 after a summer in the North American Soccer City League with Philadelphia Furies, he moved on to Birmingham City for £150,000. He top-scored there and helped them win promotion, before moves to Leeds United and Sunderland. The First Division welcomed him back with Southampton before spells with Brighton, Tranmere (as player-manager), Preston and Stockport County.

One of the games most gifted and colourful strikers, he made 757 League appearances in a career that saw him approaching his fortieth birthday before he left the first-class game.

Charlie Wright

Charlie Wright was without a doubt one of the biggest characters to have been seen at Burnden Park, where he served as player, coach and manager.

Glasgow-born, he began his career with Rangers, playing in 28 Reserve team games for them before moving to Workington in June 1958. In 1960 whilst completing his National Service in Hong Kong, he represented the Colony against Peru and later became their Footballer of the Year. He made 123 League appearances for Workington and in February 1963, he signed for Grimsby Town, where he made 129 appearances before moving to Charlton Athletic. He made 195 appearances for the Valiants and in June 1971, he joined the Wanderers. In 1971–72 he was an ever-present and helped the Wanderers register their best goals against record since 1925. He went on to win a Third Division championship medal with the Wanderers before a year later retiring through a continual back injury.

He remained at Bolton as Youth team coach before moving to York City, where he was manager for three years. He returned to Burnden in August 1981, firstly as Reserve team coach before following John McGovern's departure in January 1985, he was put in temporary charge.

Within three weeks, he had steered the Whites to five consecutive successes, their best winning sequence in six years and despite a number of applications from experienced managers, he was named Bolton manager on 7 February 1985. Incredibly, the Wanderers won only one of their next ten games, but avoided relegation thanks to an improved run during April.

In December 1985, he left the club by mutual consent after ending his Bolton career in exactly the opposite way to which it had started with five consecutive defeats!

Bolton's full league record under Charlie Wright is:

P	W	D	L	F	A
39	10	7	22	42	67

Zingari

In 1884–85, the Wanderers drew Preston Zingari in the F.A. Cup, but as both clubs were embroiled in the political issue of professionalism, they withdrew from the competition.

Acknowledgements

The author wishes to thank the following for their help in producing this book.

The officials of Bolton Wanderers Football Club; The Association of Football Statisticians and the *Bolton Evening News*. Thanks are also due to individuals: Simon Marland (Official Statistician at Bolton Wanderers F.C.) David Higson, Lindsay Frost, Elaine Hayes and Ben Hayes.

Also to Alistair Hodge and Alan Crosby of Carnegie Publishing for supporting this A–Z series.

List of Illustrations

Illustrations were kindly supplied by the *Bolton Evening News* and *Bolton Metro News*. We are grateful to the *Evening News* for Burnden Park; Ian Greaves; Freddie Hill; Eddie Hopkinson; Nat Lofthouse; Bill Ridding and Frank Worthington. To the *Metro News* for Phil Brown; John McGinlay; Julian Darby and Bruce Rioch. To Barry Taylor for Jack Milsom; Harry Goslin; Ray Westwood; Harold Blackmore; Pikes Lane; and action from the various F.A. Cup Finals of the 1920s.

To Peter Stafford for the cigarette cards and to two former Bolton internationals, Tommy Banks and Ray Parry, and finally Elaine Hayes for the Burnden Disaster.